Michael

The body,
Spirit & Soul
never sleeps. The body
rest while creation continu
to work through your thoug
you create your spirit so you
Can manifest it through your
thoughts, words & Actions.

Phoenix
John McLaughlin
3/18/2017

This book may be ordered by e-mail at: John@bodyspiritsoul77.com or

By Website at: www. bodyspiritsoul77.com

Because of the dynamic nature of the Internet, any web addresses or links contained in this book may have changed since publication and may no longer be valid. The views expressed in this work are solely those of the author.

The author of this book does not dispense medical advice or prescribe the use of any technique as a form of treatment for physical, emotional or medical problems without the advice of a physician, either directly or indirectly. The intent of the author is only to offer information of a general nature to help his readers in their quest for emotional and spiritual well-being. In the event the reader(s) use any of the information contained in this book for themselves, which is their constitutional right, the author (and publisher) assume no responsibility for the reader(s) actions or outcome.

Any people depicted in stock imagery are provided by: Imagine Design, and are being used for illustrative purposes only.

This is the first written edition of the book "An Introduction to Creation – It's Law, Processes, Rules and Realities"

FIRST EDITION: October 2015

FIRST PRINTING: October 2015

SECOND PRINTING: JULY 2016

THIRD PRINTING: October 2016

I want to thank a good friend that has been instrumental in making not only this book a reality but all the books in this series of spiritual self-help books.

If it was not for all the assistance I received from Linda Donaldson of Imagine Designs I would not have such incredible book covers on all the books I have written.

She has always sustained a smile through all the very limited pieces of information I have sent her and still produced professional covers for these books

Linda - Thank you for all your help

This book is written to give the reader a basic understanding of the Law of Creation, its rules, realities and processes. This book will help you to better understand the differences between creating a better way of life (a love-based reality) and manifesting a spirit around you.

The information contained in this book comes from a deeper understanding of the Catholic Bible's prophecy "The Revelations of Christ", its book of Genesis and the parables of the New Testament. This book is about creation which is what these parts of the Bible are describing; creation and how creation works throughout our lives. This is not a rehashing of the old debate about creation being science vs. religion. It is about creating and recreating your spirit and soul; it is about the spiritual part of creation. If everything in life is about how the body, spirit and soul exist in life; the past debates and discussion about creation have only centered on the physical aspects of creation. This book is about how the spirit and soul manifest the reality that is life.

For example:
> When you recreate your spirit and soul you can live your life with a spirit that shines with light and shares its light with you. A light-based spirit makes you feel love in your heart. A dark spirit allows you to feel anger in your day-to-day life.

The reader will learn the difference between your personal spirit and soul and the essence of who you are.

The reader will learn the fundamentals of creation and how we re-create our spirit and soul as we grow from a dark spirit to a light spirit to a bright spirit and then finally into God consciousness. As well you will understand what the collective spirit and consciousness is and how it works through you and how you can impact it.

To try to explain how creation works or how our spirit and soul work together within and around our body is not as easy as one might think. In order to understand it you have read with your eyes and ears but allow your spirit to help you to perceive the truth. It is how you perceive the world around you that is going to shape your personal realities in life. As a person learns to accept that life is a perception of their own reality then you will be capable of understanding how creation works through your body, spirit and soul.

This book is written with the intention to help you to open your mind as well as open your spiritual eyes and ears. With your spiritual eyes and ears open you can perceive a greater understanding of your life, creation and consciousness.

LIFE AND HOW THE BODY, SPIRIT AND SOUL WORK TOGETHER

Life is about living with my spirit.

The reality that is my life is a reflection of my spirit.

Life is about living with our collective spirits.

The reality of life is a reflection of our collective spirits.

The reality of my life improves as my spirit evolves into a greater light. The evolution into a lighter spirit is natural; creation and evolution are a states of nature.

My thoughts, words and actions combined with the emotion of those words that comes naturally from within me create the spirit of my thoughts, words and actions. It is more than just choosing the right words to use to create a vibration in the air around me. It is about the positive or negative nature of my spirit that will come through every cell in my body through the words I speak that will shape the spirit of my words. Your words merely facilitate the process of creation that creates the spirit of your words.

To simply choose words that sound better will not change the reality of my life. Making the world a better place for our children takes more than just choosing words that sound pretty or better than other words. The words we choose create a physical vibration in the air around us; and this is the science and physics of vibrations. But the metaphysics (means beyond physics) of the spirit of the words we use is a very different reality.

The metaphysics of the spirit of the words we use is about our personal spirit and its capability to create a positive vibration that comes from within you, from your spirit.

When a person has an intention to do something, the positive or negative nature of the intention fills our spirit with the feeling of this intention. We are then motivated to act on these feelings. Then the thoughts that guide our actions come from our soul. When we act on these feelings we create the spirit of our thoughts, words and actions. The spirit of our words comes from the pit of our stomach and out our mouth. It is the depth of emotion that we allow to come out of us that will determine the size or strength of the spirit of our words. This is the power of intention. The spirit of our words then fills the spirit of the room we are in. Every action works the same way as the positive or negative nature of the spirit of our intention fills the road we are driving on when we experience road rage or on the golf course when we hit a bad shot and experience fairway rage.

By living a life filled with love and forgiveness you create a stronger and healthier spirit than if you do not forgive those that have hurt you in the past.

To have no remorse for the hurtful actions you do to others, Is to live a life filled with a spirit that has what is referred to as a spirit sealed into a darker reality. A person that does not care about others or the hurtful things they do to others is simply a person that has an uncaring spirit. The thoughts, words and actions of a person with an uncaring spirit will create the spirit of his or her words that are uncaring. It is not about the words they choose but the reality of creation that comes from their personal spirit.

A person with a caring spirit is capable of creating loving spirit can choose to create from an anger based intention or a love based intention. But a person that shows no remorse for the things that he or she has done or cannot forgive those that have hurt him or her in the past is not capable of the same choices. A person not capable of living with love is said to be sealed in a darker reality. There are no magic wands that will release these seals. The release of these seals comes from the work you do to forgive those that you were not able to forgive in the past.

People live in an emotionally hurtful environments and have emotionally painful and traumatic events in their lives. When a person experiences these environments and events and get to a point when the pain and suffering become so great that they can no longer forgive those that create the pain in their lives they create a seal in their spirit that seals their fate.

When you reach deep into the emotions of your spirit, deep into the pit of your stomach and say, "I will never forgive" or "I hate that person so much that I will never forgive him or her for what he or she has done to me" a seal is created that prevent you from accessing the love that used to exist in your life.

This is how creation works.

To release this seal you have to forgive the person that did this unforgiveable act to you. To release the seal that now seals your fate you have to use an amount of love equal to the amount of anger or hatred you used when you said you would never forgive him or her.

A person with a loving spirit will attract others with a love-based spirit. A person with an angry spirit will attract others with an anger-based spirit. When a person releases his or her seals they will become capable of creating a better reality for themselves.

This is just simply how creation works. We create seals and then we have to release them.

This is how we create our spirit and then re-create it.

This is how we limit our potential to create love and light with every thought, word and action in our lives.

This is how we re-create our spirit so we can change the reality of our lives.

PREFACE

This book is about creation and how it works through us in our day to day lives. This book is **NOT** about the ongoing debate about science and religion and did God create the physical earth or was there an explosion that triggered a molecular chain reaction that started the universe.

This book is about you and me and how God created a world that is filled with the spirit of our intentions, emotions, thoughts, words and actions.

It is about the spirit and soul; your spirit and soul; and how we exist in a body, with a spirit and a soul.

It is about our spirit and soul's journey into an existence when it is not capable of holding light and we are not capable of living with love in our hearts; and our quest to heal and rebuild a broken spirit and soul so we can live whole again as one in body, spirit and soul. After reading this book you will understand this process as a healing process that helps a youthful immature spirit and soul evolve into a higher consciousness that has its base in a spirit that is more mature than it was in the beginning.

It is important to understand how our spirit and soul exists in our lives. The best way to envision this is to think about a cloud with an angel or loved one in the after-life sitting on it. The cloud is the spirit and the loved one in the after-life is the soul. The cloud or spirit connects us to feelings and emotions, the soul connects us to thoughts and consciousness. Consciousness is a state of knowing right and wrong; an awareness of what we need to know when we need to know it.

When our cloud or spirit is dark we live in a different reality than when it is light. It is the difference between an anger-based reality and a love-based reality. A spirit that is filled with a bright light will allow us to sense, feel, hear and just know things from a different and more clear state of mind than an anger-based state of mind.

As you read this book you will learn that there are different states of mind and different realities associated with each state of mind in which a person lives.

You will learn that your personal intentions in life will determine the reality in which you live. There are two ways to look at intention:

1) Your stated intention
2) Your personal or spiritual intention that comes from within you.

Your journey or quest into a better reality in body, spirit and soul is about how the spirit of nature creates a love-based spirit that allows you to live in a healthier reality and brings a higher consciousness through your soul's awareness of love-based consciousness.

INTRODUCTION

In the beginning God created nature and creation; then nature and creation did the rest.

In the beginning God created the Heavens. This was done so all spirit would have a place to exist separate from the body. This allows our spirit the opportunity to learn to grow from a spirit that is not capable of holding light, to one that is capable of holding light and maintaining a bright light. This was done so our spirit and soul can eventually develop into the white light of God consciousness. God consciousness is a state of being where the body, spirit and soul and the essence of who you are exist as one being of pure consciousness.

In the beginning there was the spirit of man.

In the beginning God breathed life into the soul of man and a complete being was formed.

In the beginning your spirit and soul fed off of the knowledge of good and evil.

In the beginning Adam and Eve (the spirit and soul of mankind) were clothed in skin.

In the beginning Cane and Abel created through envy and the spirit of nature began its creations.

In the beginning man created the darkness that we are now just beginning to transform into light.

The law of creation is very simple:

"We must all always strive to create light.
We must all always strive to love completely.
We must always share that love with others by living with light in our spirits, love in our hearts and creating high quality relationships with others."

As we live our day-to-day lives we should love completely. We love completely by living with passion. Living with passion is about loving everything we do and everyone we meet with all our heart, soul, mind and strength.

The spirit and soul of mankind existed in a place called Eden until it fed off the knowledge of good and evil. Then it was clothed in skin so the spirit and soul would have the experiences needed to learn about both.

Creation is about how we re-create our spirit and soul as we transform them from an anger-based consciousness to a love-based consciousness.

This is why it is so important that we learn to love again.

Love is the key; love is the answer. To re-create your spirit into a love-based spirit is the key to transforming your soul so you can live with love-based consciousness.

We are all here to learn how anger feels so we can receive that something, the oomph or commitment to changing our life, that is deep inside all of us. A deep-rooted commitment is what we need to motivate us to change and to grow. As we grow we are literally transforming our spirit. As our spirit becomes stronger it becomes capable of holding light; we then feel better about our-selves.

CREATING

When we feel this deep connection to the love our soul feeds us. Our soul feeds us what we need to know in order to maintain light in our spirit and love in our heart.

As we learn to create a better life for our-selves we will also learn to co-create better relationships through others.

It is through love-based relationships that we will co-create through the sharing of a common interest, common intention and purpose in life. As we learn the power that intention plays in our lives we will learn to create and co-create peace of mind and then just let peace on earth exist in the air all around us.

Specifically, what we create is the spirit of our personal intention, the emotion we feel and commit to this creation and the essence of that which we are at the moment of creation. The spirit of that which we create contains that which we are at the moment of creation.

The components of the process of creation and all creations are:

The spirit of our emotions
The spirit of our intention
The spirit of our intentions and emotions glow through our thoughts, words and actions
The essence of our state of mind at the moment of creation when our intentions, emotions (depth of commitment which is a function of our intention), thoughts, words and actions combine to create the spirit of who we are at that moment

The emotions that combine with our intention when we think, say or do anything and everything in our lives

- When our spirit and soul are both healthy and strong we no longer create through the essence of our state of mind. With a healthy spirit and soul we create through our personal essence.

We are creating the spirit of our thoughts, words and actions all day long every day.

With every word we speak we create the spirit of our words. The compassion, sympathy, love, respect, anger or disrespect that accompanies our words combines with our intention to create the spirit of our words. The essence of a darker state of mind might be the essence of greed, lust, gluttony, sloth, pride or envy.

Did you ever listen to a friend and feel the spirit of his or her words?

Did you ever feel the tone of an email or letter you received from a friend or co-worker?

Stop sometime and feel the words that come from a CNN or FOX News pundit as he or she shouts at their audience?

Please learn to understand that a lot of the feelings you feel from someone are the feelings they are projecting with the spirit of their words; they may not be your personal feelings.

Someday listen to the words one person says to you and then think about how you feel. Then listen to the same words that come from another person and see if there is a difference in how the two different people make you feel. Even though their words were the same the spirit of these words may be different.

It is the personal intention of the two different people that will create a different feeling within you.

A person with a positive and caring intention will make you feel positive about yourself.

A person with a negative intention will make you feel negative or angry after you listen to what they have to say.

A person's intention will determine the positive or negative spirit that will be created through your relationship with him or her. A person's words may be very positive but the spirit of the words will be anger based. It is the person's spiritual base that will determine the love or anger the person is possible of creating from. Then the spirit of his or her words will be a reflection of the essence of his spirit of the essence of his state of mind.

WHY DOES THE SPIRIT AND SOUL HAVE A HUMAN EXPERIENCE

Did you ever meet someone that you could just tell lives with a lot of anger in his or her life?

Did you ever wonder if that person was stuck and would have to live with anger for the rest of his life?

Life is all about the spirit and soul having a human experience. These experiences last many lifetimes. In the beginning our spirit entered this physical world as a much darker spirit than any of us are today. As we live with a darker spirit we create the collective spirit of mankind and manifest the ambient spirit of the world. Then as we grow out of the darkness of our self we re-create and transform the darkness of our individual spirit, collective spirit and manifest a love-based ambient spirit as we all grow from dark to light to bright and then finally to God. This is the reason for the spirit and soul's human experience.

The goal or end game of our physical life and spiritual existence is to transform our spirit and soul from an existence without light (living in dark) to living in God. The goal is to create a spirit and soul as one with God, with God's spirit in our day to day lives and to allow God's Will on earth. God's Will on earth is the reality that exists in the world. The dark and lightness of the collective spirit is a reflection of the reality that is life on earth. God's Will is that the collective spirit and soul constantly change. This change is designed to bring a greater light through the collective spirit and soul; thereby making the world a better place.

To accomplish this we have to grow through various states of mind and levels of consciousness. The various levels of consciousness are:

1) I Need Consciousness
2) I Am Consciousness
3) We Are Consciousness
4) We Are Us Consciousness
5) We Are God Consciousness

"I NEED" CONSCIOUSNESS

In the "I Need" consciousness people strive to survive and to control their lives. In this state of mind cravings, desires, wants and needs tend to rule your life. When you feel like your life is out of control you will strive to regain control by using things and other people. Having things and associating with the right people can become paramount in your life. You live as if you have to have the best toys or the right people in your life. Some people just have to fit-in with the right people. Life does not have to be about having the right people in your life, in higher levels of consciousness it is about relationships, it is about having quality relationships that create a positive bond between you and the other person, it is a about bond with a foundation in a shared purpose.

When in this "I Need" Consciousness you will feel as if you cannot stop yourself from doing things that you know deep down are wrong but you feel a strong need or desire to do it anyways. This state of consciousness is about shaping other people's opinions of you. You feel as if you have to measure up to a standard that others set for you or for them-selves and you have to compete to be like those around you. You strive to make sure you say and do the right things in order to shape their opinions of you. Your thoughts will allow you to rationalize that it is acceptable to lie, manipulate and deceive others into believing what you say and do as you try to shape and form their opinion of you. The reality of this state of mind is that your spirit does not hold light in it. When you start to learn how to transform your spirit so it can hold light, you will learn how to live with light in your spirit, love in your heart and the power that comes with it. In this state of mind you want everyone to work for you; even your spirit works for you. For some people in this state of mind, even their spirit is supposed to do what it is told to do.

"I AM" CONSCIOUSNESS

The "I Am" consciousness comes with the realization that you do not have to let cravings, desires or wants and needs rule your life; a sense of freedom to live how you want to live enters your spirit. It is when you become aware of your spirit and that you can become one with it; that you find a sense of love for your-self in your life. This brings a completely new reality into your life. It is natural to try to use your spirit, God, the Universe and Creation to work for you by intentionally manifesting things into your life in an attempt to make your life easier or better for you. As you evolve beyond this level of consciousness you will no longer have any wants or needs in your life, no desires to have things or people in the physical as your reality shifts into a higher spiritual reality and consciousness. This level of consciousness is about becoming aware of who you are as a person that has a greater potential. It is about learning to just be you; instead of trying to be the person you want others to think you are.

"WE ARE" CONSCIOUSNESS

The "We Are" consciousness is a reality shift that brings with it an awareness of our true power to use our spirit and soul to make the world a better place. It is the awareness that we no longer need anything the world has to offer because we love others completely. Instead of a need to have things and people in our lives we realize that all we need is to have quality relationships with our-self (our personal spirit and soul) and others. As we accept others for who they are they will genuinely accept us for who we are (this is how creation works). We begin to realize, with the true power of creation comes realities like acceptance. Being accepted by others is a function of how openly I accept others for who they are. It is an understanding that my intention in life is about how I live my life not what I want to manifest in my life so I can make my life easier to live. It is the realization that I live my life and create through how I share my love and the power of my intention to create love-based relationships with everyone I meet. This is what will make my life easier to live. Life becomes easier to live when I create love through my interactions with others. As we live in this "We Are Consciousness" we grow into a state of mind where we sense and feel those that are close to us and we have a sense of being connected to them. There are times when we will hear a friend's thoughts or feel their feelings, when we will feel a sense of unison or being at one with close personal friends or family. This sense of one-ness comes with a sense of sincerity in our personal intention.

"WE ARE US" CONSCIOUSNESS

The "We Are Us" consciousness prepares you to learn how to allow God, Nature and Creation to work through you. At this level of consciousness you begin to understand the collective consciousness and you begin to live with a reality that is very different. In this reality you begin to recognize the importance of having purposeful love-based relationships. It is the quality of your relationships that is important. In the "I Am Consciousness" you build a relationship with your-self (between your body and your spirit). In this higher level you use the love you now feel with your body and spirit connection to make (or produce) better relationships with others. First it will begin with friends and family as it then grows into better relationships with the community around you. It begins with friends from our own age group because we all come into this world connected to the generation of people that we are born with. A generation is about 20 – 22 year period of time where a group of children enters the world with a greater love than the previous generation; and a purpose to use the love in their spirit to make the world a better place. As we connect to the spirit and purpose of our generation we are growing into the "We Are Us Consciousness" and the reality of our lives shifts once again. With this shift comes a feeling of just letting go of the control we have in our lives and just let God work through us. As we learn to let a feeling of purpose guide our thoughts, words and actions (create through us) we are learning to give up control over our lives and let God guide us. If you think about the progression from the "I Need Consciousness" to this higher level of consciousness; we all have to experience life at these lower levels and then learn these lessons before we will be able to just let God work through us. If there was a magic wand that just instantaneously transformed us from the lowest level to God overnight it would be very traumatic for our spirits and souls. At this "We Are Us" level, our spirits are more connected to one another as we start to work together with rhythm and harmony as a family and community. Collectively there is less judgment in the world. A greater sense of balance will accompany the oneness that is the "We Are Us" Consciousness.

"WE ARE GOD" CONSCIOUSNESS

The "We Are God" consciousness is the culmination of many lifetimes of work as we strive to mend a broken spirit and soul and grow from the controlling realities of a darker spirit into the sharing and acceptance-based realties of love and light. In the lower levels of consciousness the realities we lived in were based on how we control our lives thereby preventing love and light from working through us. As we learned to love we create love for ourselves and for others. As we learn to accept that WE ARE GOD (not I am God) but that we the collective spirit and consciousness of mankind are God we learn to accept God into our spirit again. This creates the greatest understanding of the reality that all is good. Judgment leaves our consciousness as it is replaced with acceptance, peace of mind and wisdom.

We are here to learn how to live with a spirit that is capable of holding light so we could allow ourselves to connect with us; thereby creating the love and light that is God. As we grow into a greater comfort with having a sincere intention in our lives we make better relationships with others. Through purpose-filled, love-based relationships we find a sense of closeness in our spirit; this allows us to feel comfortable letting go of our need to have things and people in our lives.

When we feel like it is normal to need things and people in our lives to feel good about our life we are in the lower levels of consciousness. When it feels like it is just human nature to use people as if it is acceptable to manipulate and deceive others with our words we are in these lower levels of consciousness and live with a spirit that exists in a darker state of mind. As we grow our spirit to have the strength to allow a love for others to just flow though us we are entering a higher spiritual state and consciousness. With this sense of comfort with others and the spiritual development that comes with it we will feel more comfortable being one with all; letting God enter our spirit.

A new sense of purpose grows in you as you accept that God created you for a reason and a purpose. As your spirit and soul become a stronger part of your life this sense of purpose will just be there. As you are living this purposeful life you will now be able to just let God come through you as you become one with God through your spiritual purpose in life. As your personal essence becomes a reality in your life and existence you are becoming one as God and in God.

We all have a spirit, soul and essence with its own unique rhythm and vibration. With this rhythm and vibration comes a purpose that is unique to you. As this feeling of just letting go and letting God enters your life you will finally feel comfortable just being you. As you live with God as one among many that just love and accept life as it is. With acceptance comes a sense of peacefulness and calmness that will exist amid the chaos of life. It is not about the world changing around you – it is about you changing how you feel about the world around you, it is about how you become more capable of living with the chaos that is the world around you as you now strive to make the world a better place for all.

How we become one in body, spirit and soul is through evolution. We dis-evolved from the beginning as Adam and Eve and we will evolve into one again. Lifetime after lifetime the broken spirit that was Adam has evolved into the many souls that exist in the world today. We are the broken spirit that is mankind. Now through the healing that is taking place lifetime after lifetime we are going to evolve into one again. Generation after generation and life time after lifetime we are evolving into a healthier spirit. Eventually there will be a time when we will become one again in body, spirit and soul. In this state of oneness we will exist and be tested to make sure that we will not fall asleep or be overcome by the wants and needs of a physical existence. After living as one body, spirit and soul we will then continue our existence as the healed essence of who we are as God.

PART 1

A HEALTHY AND UNHEALTHY BODY, SPIRIT AND SOUL

CREATION vs MANIFESTATION

A healthy body, spirit and soul is a state of existence in which the mind and the body function as one. This is the being or beacon of light in which many people speak of. It is a life in which the body spirit and soul allows the essence of a person to exist in your day to day life and lives.

A healthy spiritual life is one in which the body, spirit and soul are so in tune with one another that a person merely feels a feeling then knows the appropriate response to that feeling. It is not about listening to a person's words and then responding in a way that is most appropriate for the situation.

When we are one in body, spirit and soul we trust the intuition of our feelings and thoughts as we express our true feelings for the sole purpose of just being who we are not who we want the world to think we are.
When we live to convince others that we are someone that they should like or acknowledge we are manifesting the person we want to be.

When we simply know who we are and tell people what we feel and think, we are creating from the source of creation. We create relationships that are real and true because they are based on our true feelings and they come from our heart not just the words that are needed to get what we want in life.

A HEALTHY AND UNHEALTHY BODY, SPIRIT AND SOUL

In the physical we live, eat and breathe our realities based on time. Today's reality is a function of what we are going to do in the waking hours of the day. The reality we create is a function of what we did yesterday and want to do tomorrow. Our reality also is a function of our emotional health and well-being which is directly linked to our spiritual health and well-being. Spiritual health and well-being is a function of our spirit's strength or ability to hold light. When our spirit is consumed by light we will feel love. When it is consumed by darkness we will feel anger, hatred, rage, ire, distain or wrath. When we are not able to feel love at all there is an emotional block that exists within us that prevents us from being capable of feeling love. All the colors of the spectrum from white through red, orange, yellow, green, blue, violet, purple and all shades of gray and black have a specific vibration associated with them. Our spirit also has a vibration specific to it. We are capable of living with a spirit that is any or all of these energetic vibrations throughout our life. When our spirit is unhealthy it is too weak to hold the vibrations that are represented by the colors of the rainbow or white. An unhealthy spirit is not capable of holding these higher vibrating energies. Darker colors like gray and black are considered lower vibrating energies. Light and dark energies are polar opposites of one another and generate feelings within us that are also polar opposites; like love and anger comes from light and dark energies, respectively. When our spirit is not capable of holding a positive vibration we are sealed away from feeling love and the conscious awareness that comes with it. Since we react to our feelings we will naturally live with a reality that is created through anger or love depending on the health and well-being of our spirit. Anger becomes a driving force in our physical reality until we can create a meta-physical change in our spirit's reality.

In spirit our reality is a function of what our spirit and soul is or is not consumed by. A healthy spirit will be consumed by our Will to accomplish a goal or purpose. An unhealthy spirit might be consumed by the essence of greed, lust or gluttony that motivates a person's actions and behaviors. If we are experiencing love at one moment in time our spirit will have a love-based experience. If we are experiencing anger our spirit will exist in that moment with a darkness that is a reflection of the anger that created it. If we are depressed our spirit will experience a lack of life as if it is asleep (this is often referred to as being dead to creation). When we have an unhealthy spirit we are not capable of experiencing our life with a certain range of thoughts, feelings and emotions. When we go from being happy go lucky one minute to being filled with anger, hatred or rage the next it may be because our spirit is not capable of holding the light needed to express our self in any other way. If we lose our ability to love we lose our ability to cope with a lot of situations through love and compassion. Without love in our lives our spirit is not capable of allowing us to express love to others. When someone says the words, "I just don't care" it will immediately create a spirit that just does not care; or if a person's spirit is not capable of caring, he or she may say, "I just don't care".

A person whose spirit cannot experience love and light at all may not even be able to say the words, "I love you". This is our spirit and soul's reality. These are the reasons why it is important to think about our spiritual health and live to create a spiritually healthy life. With a spiritually healthy life our spirit can exist in our lives in such a way as to allow us to be consumed by the light and love of our spirit's reality every single moment of every single day.

A person with a healthy body, spirit and soul will never feel consumed by any emotion or reality that does not come from within him or her. This is because he or she is constantly experiencing and expressing all the emotions they feel. When our body, spirit and soul is capable of processing a full range of light and dark energy into feelings and emotions and then expressing these emotions in our day-to-day lives we are living a spiritually healthy existence. It is when we are not capable of experiencing or expressing an emotion or a range of emotions that our spirit and soul will have an unhealthy existence; and we will experience life with emotional problems. Until we address emotional problems from the perspective of re-creating our spirit we never fully understand the problem or its solutions. This is why we continue to treat spiritual problems with drugs (both recreational and prescribed), alcohol and behaviors that are designed to consume our spirit. When a person does anything to an extreme it is because this extreme behavior is necessary to make the person either feel something or suppress the feelings they wish to deny. When our spiritual reality is such that it is easier to live our life in denial of our spiritual reality we will do things like exercise to an extreme, live with sex, drug and alcohol addictions, and other behaviors that force our body to reject our life's reality.

For example when our spirit is consumed by anger and our soul is filled with memories of past experiences that we are not ready to deal with. People that live in this reality need to create a life for themselves that will allow them to live with fewer of these feelings and memories. So they turn to drugs, alcohol, sex, work or exercise. People that are obsessed with exercise or sex are using it to suppress these hurtful feelings and thoughts (memories). They use sex and exercise in the same way that many use drugs and alcohol for the same purpose. Our spirit needs to share these feelings with us so we can cleanse the darkness of these feelings from within it. When these feelings seem like they will overwhelm us we need to do something that will help us to live without them. This is when we turn to drugs, alcohol, sex and other behaviors that will consume our day-to-day life so we can contain and control the rage that exists' in our personal spirit.

When people see behaviors in others (especially children) that make them feel uncomfortable they immediately label the other person as sick and then a medical practitioner diagnoses the behaviors and prescribes a behavior altering drug. These drugs then impact a person's body chemistry in such a way as to allow the person to present themselves in a way that is more socially acceptable. Then those that could not deal with these behaviors in the first place will feel better. When these drugs then impact the body's chemistry they also impact the spirit's ability to exist in the person's day-to-day life. This makes the person feel less or not feel at all. Some people may say their stomach feels funny or they just feel weird and out of place when taking these mood altering drugs. They alter the mood because they prevent the spirit and its feelings from being an active part of the person's life.

I am not trying to say that mood altering prescription drugs are wrong. I am trying to say that they are not solving the problem. They do not allow the person that came into this world to learn about the reality in their life that creates these behaviors. These drugs should only be used as a stop gap measure to help a person learn to control or correct the problems and issues that relate to emotional problems that present them-selves as the result of an unhealthy spirit.

CREATION vs. MANIFESTATION

We create through the natural process of creation that comes from God's creation. Creation is a process that allows your personal intention to flow from within you. Creation creates the new reality that is your life. A naturally sincere intention will create a different reality than an insincere intention. A sincere intention comes from a strong personal spirit; from a person's that is strong enough to be sincere. A weaker spirit is only capable of less sincere intentions. A weaker spirit replaces sincerity with deceiving and manipulating.

CREATION

Creation is a natural process that exists in nature and creation. These processes were originally created for the body, spirit and soul to have a human experience. It is only through a human experience that an unhealthy spirit can and will create the motivation needed to transform itself.

The end goal to creation is to be able to create a new reality for you. This is a new reality in your life. The key to doing this is to be able to gain access to a greater consciousness. A greater consciousness comes from the spirit being capable of processing a greater light (a brighter light) into it and then your soul becomes capable of accessing new awareness. With this new light in your spirit and awareness coming from your soul, you become capable of knowing and doing things differently. This is how our spirit and soul becomes healthier. A greater consciousness is sort of like having a book in your mind and you read it chapter by chapter. As your spirit grows into a new light then another chapter is open to you. Your consciousness grows as you learn to accept new thoughts that come from it. As you apply what you learn from the chapters of the book your consciousness is reading; you are learning to live in your new reality. As you read and apply the new chapter, you will then be able to grow your spirit into a greater light so you can then gain access to the next chapter. As you continue to change into this new you, it will seem like you never changed at all it will be like this new reality is normal, as if you always knew this was the right way to live. Your friends and family will notice the change. You will feel more comfortable talking about things you used to deny were a part of your life. This process of developing your spirit and soul is what spiritual development is all about.

Before a person can grow into the light side of the heavens and access this knowledge or awareness of a different reality, you must first shift from a dark reality into the light. The only path from dark to light is through the process of forgiveness. To forgive and live with love is to open the doors to the bookstore that will allow you to access the knowledge or awareness that comes from this book of enlightenment. The process of forgiveness and living with love will recreate your spirit thereby causing a shift in your life's reality. To re-create a spirit is to change its polarity from dark to light. This is what a shift or a lifting of a veil is all about. After re-creating a spirit and soul, a person can then change his or her life into a love-based reality. As a person shares this love with others, an even more powerful change occurs, as the powers of the process of co-creation exist in this person's life, in the collective consciousness of mankind and in the ambient spirit of the world. We can then manifest a new reality for all of mankind. This new reality is the greater collective consciousness that comes with a new human nature.

Throughout this book we will talk a lot about love. The love(s) we are discussing are not about romantic love. These loves come with the spirit of the kingdom of the heavens and are used for the purpose of creation. Romantic love is what mankind has manifested for many, many thousands of years. When love comes from the kingdom of the heavens it flows through us and into the world around us. It is a feeling we receive and an emotion that flows through us. The process of creating through the kingdom of the heavens is very similar to manifesting but is very different because the spirit of love that comes from these heavens is not romantic love. Love from the heavens is a more pure love because it comes from God's creation not from man's manifestation. Unconditional love is to just love and accept others no matter who they are or what they do to you or your friends and family. It comes with an awareness that all is good. Love brings with it the ability to just naturally forgive those that wish you harm.

MANIFESTATION

Many thousands of years ago the ancient prophets referred to manifesting. When they talked about manifesting they were talking about how our spirit and soul manifests the reality that is our life. They also talked about how the collective spirit and collective consciousness manifested the way of life that existed. Today, many people have redefined manifestation and creation in such a way as to mean that we are supposed to use our spirit to make something that we need appear in our lives. By using our spirit as if it is a slave to do our bidding is a way of forcing or using our will to meet a want or need. This is very different from the definition of manifestation that existed in the days of the ancient prophets.

Manifestation is a reality that mankind has been doing for thousands of years. Today, manifestation is defined as, how we use or manipulate the forces of creation in such a way as to manifest something we want or need. It is how we assert our will in such a way as to use nature to work for us. A manifestation can be something physical, emotional or spiritual.

Physical
Some people have successfully manifested many different kinds of objects into their life by simply praying for them or asking the universe to provide them. Many people have also been very unsuccessful at manifesting their wants and needs.

Emotional
Most people have even been successful at manifesting emotions into their spirit. To manifest an emotion is about having an intention to no longer be sad or angry and then to ask God, the Universe or Mother Nature to then take away the sadness or anger.

Spiritual
Some people then manifest a positive spirit around them (many call this a white light of protection) as they strive to survive and feel better in the reality that is their life. Quite often, this is the first step for many people as they walk their path into the light side of the kingdom of the heavens. This is about manifesting a new spirit or vibration into or around your spirit so you can express yourself through it instead of expressing yourself through anger or sadness of your reality. You will not gain access to the knowledge of love and light that comes from re-creating your spirit but you will feel a little better from time to time.

While using these manifesting techniques your root feelings of sadness and anger will still exist in your life. Manifesting a spirit into your life is only modifying your spirit not changing it. You still create through the sadness of anger that is in your personal spirit. It is only masked by what you manifested. To manipulate your reality is to have an intention to make your life better. This intention is a good thing and will help you on your quest to create a better life for yourself.

To manifest a spirit that you can use in your day-to-day life will not change the reality of your day-to-day life. A reality shift will only occur after learning the process of forgive and live with love. To modify your spirit is to allow this other spirit to exist in it until you are ready to forgive. After you have experienced the process of forgiveness, you will no longer need this manifested spirit.

Today many people define manifestation as the use of an intention and a commitment to it through the forces of nature and creation to bring something into your life. For example, when a person prays for a new car and is then guided to drive a new direction home from work; then they see the exact car they want for the right price. It was more than just the prayer but also accepting the guidance that comes from the spirit of the prayer. The stronger your commitment to what you want to manifest, the stronger the spirit you will create; but you also have to accept the guidance it offers. Others have asked for a car and when presented with the guidance (thoughts that guide you to do something that will help you manifest this new car) to drive past the new car; they reject the thoughts that encourage them to drive a new way home. This just creates confusion in the spirit of your manifestation. However, spirit will be as persistent as you are committed to this manifestation. You will be encouraged through many thoughts to drive that new direction home and when you finally do, you will see your car and stop. Now what happens to many people is, when they look at the car and they see it is a good car and the right price; but now they slip into a different mode of thinking and critique it for color and options. Suddenly the perfect car turns into a car that is the wrong color or does not have an option they now believe they need etc. This now adds even more confusion to the spirit of that which they strive to manifest. As this process of confusion continues to grow in the spirit of the request this person asks for a new car. The spirit of this request now grows weaker and weaker until it eventually dissipates. As it grows weaker and dissipates, anxiety and frustration, replace the good feelings that were originally committed to it. When people have a lack of confidence they struggle with trusting their intuition and the guidance that comes with it. This reality of wanting and needing and then not accepting the happiness you are looking for is how your spirit feeds and feeds off the need to be sad

Manifestation and Creation have several things in common. They both use an intention to make a change in your life. Both Creation and Manifestation work through prayers and use nature and creation to help us to live our lives.

THE DIFFERENCE BETWEEN MANIFESTATION AND CREATION AS DEFINED IN RECENT YEARS IS:

CREATION

Creation is a natural process that just happens in our life. It is not something we control.

Creation uses the intention and emotion that comes from you naturally to manifest the spirit of who you are at the moment of creation. This intention and emotion is a reflection of you, of who you are at the moment of creation.

When people live with the pain and suffering of a darker spirit they still feel and act on love. It is not the same love or the same manifestation as people that live with a light-based spirit. When people in a darker reality live with fear-based feelings and emotions they will manifest their love throughout their day to day lives. In people with lesser light or no light love manifests as a controlling personality or as a self-centered realty where they are capable of sharing their life with someone who does things for them or gives them things.

Many people may know someone like this.

Like, that person that will only spend time with those that do what they want to do not what the rest of the group wants to do.

Like, those people that spend more time with a child because that child gives them something they need. It can be an emotional need or because that child will keep his or her secrets.

Like that person who tells the boss what he wants to hear and then the boss gives him or her more power and authority in the running of the business.

This is how love manifests in people that have a lesser light.

Creation happens naturally.

Love happens naturally.

Anger, hatred and rage happens naturally.

What we manifest happens naturally

Creation is not a magic wand that we can simply wave and then suddenly create a new life for ourselves; it is a lot of hard work.

Creation will create a new reality in your life.

Creation is an essential part of God's plan to transform your spirit so you can have a different reality in your life but you cannot control when it happens.

Creation is about accessing a higher conscious awareness. The higher consciousness you create is your life's reality; it is a function of the emotion that you are capable of living with.

Creation is about using the love or anger that comes naturally to you to create the reality that is your life.

Creation uses the spirit of nature and creation to transform your spirit and soul into a higher light in the kingdom of the heavens. Today many refer to the kingdom of the heavens as Source.

Creation is about creating as environment in your life (this involves your spirit and soul) that allows the essence of your being to thrive in love and light.

THE FORGIVENESS PRAYER OR MANTRA

I want you to say this prayer or mantra for a minute.

First, do this only when you truly want to forgive someone for something they did to you. Do not do this because you want the benefits of forgiveness. This is the wrong intention. Be true to your intention, so only do this when you truly want to forgive someone. Think about a time in your life when someone close to you did something that hurt you deeply; something that was very difficult for you to forgive them for having done this to you. Remember what it was and how you felt when it happened. Remember the sadness and/or anger of the moment.

Second, I want you to think or say out loud, "I forgive you, <u>use the name off the person you are thinking about</u>!!! Now reach deep inside of you and feel as much love for this person as you can and say, "I forgive you" again. Continue saying, "I forgive you" with as much love for this person as possible each time. You should be able to feel the sadness and anger leaving you as you do this over and over again. Say this as many times as you feel is appropriate.

Continue Doing this mantra or prayer several times a day until you start to feel very deep emotional moments throughout your day. These deep emotions should be new emotions not the same feelings you have felt throughout your life. These are the emotions you lost when you were not able to forgive the person who hurt you. Then with these added emotions forgive him of her again; use these emotions to forgive at a much deeper level. This will create a healthier spirit for you.

<u>MANIFESTATION</u>

Manifestation is the manipulation of the forces of nature and creation through a conscious intention to bring something into your life.

Manifestation is the use of the forces of creation and nature to do work for you.

Manifestation uses a stated intention and emotion to manifest a want or need.

Manifestation will make it easier for you to live in the state of mind that your personal spirit exists in but it will not change your spirit or the reality of your life.

PART 2

CREATION AND HOW IT WORKS

GOD, THE GODS OF THE PAST, THE CATHOLIC CHURCH AND THE ROMAN EMPIRE

AN INTRODUCTION TO CREATION

THE TEN RULES OF CREATION

THE TWELVE REALITIES OF CREATION

CREATION IS WHAT GOD CREATED "IN THE BEGINNNING".

IN THE BEGINNING "DARKNESS WAS OVER THE DEEP AND THE SPIRIT OF GOD WAS OVER THE WATERS".

Creation was needed so spirit that was not capable of holding light could learn to transform its self from a darker anger-based spirit into a love-based spirit capable of holding light.

Once God created creation he let it be and then it made (manifested) the physical realities that we now call life. Life is the spirit and soul's human experience. Since I have a spirit that is capable of creating the spirit of my thoughts, words and actions, I am capable of creating (manifesting). This makes me a creator but does not make me God. I am only God-like. We are God and we create (manifest) the reality that is life. We are the collective spirit of mankind and we create human nature.

There are two ways of understanding the realities of creation. There are realities that come from God's intention (our collective intention) or individual intention at the moment of creation and there are realities associated with creation itself. For example there is the reality that people will exist as creators in body, spirit and soul and there is the realities related to that which we create – after the spirit of our thoughts words and actions manifest these spiritual creations want to perpetuate their existence and will feed off of us. Since we created them we have to feed them and they will strive to feed off of us. When we create the spirit of our thoughts, words and actions we create through processes of creation. These processes of creation are another reality that exists because of God's creation.

Our purpose in life is to learn to live in the realities of the world so we can transform our spirit and soul in such a way as to no longer need to live in this world. As we transform our spirit and soul into a lighter existence we will then no longer need this human experience as our spirit and soul continue on in its existence. The first spiritual reality of creation is creation itself. The second reality of creation is - in order to create light you must first live in light. The next level of creation is that in order for any one person to create through light, light must exist in the collective spirit of mankind.

There is a sense of order to the way creation is structured. For example, a first order reality is - in order for an individual to create through light he or she must first live in light.
Then a second order of creation is - in order for a person to be able to live in light there must be light in the collective spirit of mankind. The collective spirit will then feed the individual that which is a part of the collective spirit of mankind.

The third order of creation is that any person who grows a personal spirit that is greater than the collective spirit creates within the collective spirit of mankind. This is what makes spiritual leaders like Jesus, Moses, Mohammad, Gandhi and Buddha great prophets. When Jesus lived and taught others about love and forgiveness while at the same time practicing it; he created love and forgiveness in the collective spirit of mankind. When a person creates his or her personal spirit to contain the vibration of something, like forgiveness, when it does not exist within the collective spirit, he or she is creating the spirit of forgiveness in the collective spirit of mankind.

In the parables of the bible and the prophecy Revelations there is reference to the "Son of Man". The Son of Man is that which mankind creates. It is the collective spirit and soul of mankind. The collective soul is the collective consciousness. The collective spirit and soul of mankind is the sum total of all of mankind's creations throughout history. When Jesus refers to drinking his blood he is referring to a reality of creation called spiritual nourishment. To drink his blood is to fill your spirit with the vibration of love and light that he created in the collective spirit of mankind.

This chapter is about our spiritual realities and how our spiritual reality affects our personal life.

Creation is about

1) how our personal spirit exists in heaven
2) how our spirit effects or changes our life in the physical
3) how our life in the physical impacts or affects our spirit in the heavens

As we change, our spirit changes and as our spirit changes the realities that are our lives change.

When we die we leave our body and whatever state of mind our spirit is in, is a reflection of how our spirit and soul will exist until we return to try again.

There are rules that you can live by to help you to prevent your spirit from losing its capability to hold light.

These rules are the realities that we all know we need to live by but many of us struggle to accomplish them every single day of our lives.

These rules are:

STOP CREATING THROUGH A DARK SPIRIT

1) Always strive to eliminate anger from your life.
2) Always strive to eliminate lust from your life.
3) Do not make promises or deals with God – Just do the right thing in life and then let your life be what it is. If you do not like something in your life then live in a better way; a more love based way and your life will get better because you will create it, you will make it better.
4) Do not volley someone else's anger back to them. Do not seek revenge for someone else's inappropriate actions. Just turn the other cheek.
5) Love completely, especially those that wish you harm

START CREATING THE LIGHT-BASED SPIRIT FOUNDATION THAT WE ALL NEED TO LIVE WITH

6) Forgive, Forgive, Forgive – Live to practice forgiveness in all aspects of your life.
7) Love deeply in everything you say, think and do.
8) Be righteous – Always strive to just do the right thing. Live with an intention to always do what you know to be the right thing to do.
9) Give generously and be grateful as often as you possibly can.
10) Share the love you feel throughout your life with everyone you meet. Many will make sharing love their purpose in life.

There are also twelve realities of creation.

The twelve realities of creation are about how we are impacted by our spirit as we grow from dark to light and then to a bright spirit. These realities are about a spirit that survives in the darkness of anger, its consciousness and realities; and transforms into a spirit that thrives on living with light and love. A different reality exists when you feel the love of life that comes with a consciousness that feeds you through positive reinforcement. This reality is one that exists when you feed off of the positive nature of having a love-based spirit. With a weaker spirit you are always trying to tell yourself that you have to be positive or that you are going to win if you just do a little more to accomplish a goal or objective.

In order to understand creation it might help to understand how the reality of God came to be.

GOD, THE GODS OF THE PAST, THE CATHOLIC CHURCH AND THE ROMAN EMPIRE

Before explaining creation you must first understand how we have collectively expanded our understanding of God and the Creator over the past 2,000 years. There are many ways that people refer to God (god).

Some refer to God as the omnipotent creator of all that is.

Some people refer to the god's of the past – for example there were the Egyptian gods, the Roman gods, the Greek gods etc....

There are those that refer to the Supreme Being as God and others refer to God as Source (the Source of all that is).

Jesus referred to the collective spirit of mankind as the Son of Man (also Revelations explains the evolution of the spirit and soul of man through an image referred to as the Son of Man and the Seven Churches). Jesus also referred to the God of the Living and the God of the Dead. If God is the collective spirit of mankind then the God of the Living is that part of the collective sprit of mankind that exists with a light spirit in the light side of the heavens. Therefore the God of the dead is that part of the collective spirit that exists with a darker spirit and in the darker side of the heavens.

The Catholic Bible's Old Testament refers to God as The God of Jacob and Isaac and Abraham, God (in the book of Genesis), the Lord God (in Genesis) and others that are listed above. The God of Jacob and Isaac and Abraham is the spirit that manifested from the collective spirit of the tribes of the Israelites. In the same way the Roman gods, Greek gods and Egyptian gods were all manifested from the collective spirit of the people of these nations.

The Bibles book of Revelations refers to the Living god. The living god is the ambient spirit of mankind's creations that lives and changes from generation to generation and life-time to life-time. The living god is that which we manifest collectively.

To best explain how all of these references to God and god are correct and true and some are making reference to the same reality we must first go back several thousand years to a time when man was first becoming aware of the spirit of god and creation. This is a time when very few understood creation and what they knew was very limited. This is the time of the Roman gods, Greek gods, Egyptian gods, Norse gods, the god of Jacob and Isaac and Abraham and more.

The time when people felt the power of their own collective spirit is the time when people felt the presence of the god of their own tribe, country or nation. The truth is the Roman gods, Greek gods, Egyptian gods et al were the spirit that manifested as a result of the will of the people of that particular tribe, nation or country. Our power to create comes through the collective spirit of mankind not from an individual person. When people from Greece were going to war against the people for Rome the fear and anger through which they lived at that moment manifested the aggressive spirit of their god of war (Mars, Aries etc.) These gods were manifested by the collective spirit of the people that were worried about their friends and family that were going off to war and used by the warriors to fight their battles. Then as these warriors were returning the love goddesses were manifested by the spirits of the warriors returning and the women waiting for them to return. Every tribe, nation and country used to have the same gods within the collective spirit of their own culture. They could feel the power of their manifestation and feared it and used it for its purpose. Today the spirit of these cultures continues to try to exist in our day to day lives. As we feed the spirit of a holy war we perpetuate the existence of the very conflict we all hope to see end.

How do we feed this spirit of a Holy war?

By simply carrying anger or resentment towards another religion of spiritual belief system we contribute to the energy or spirit of a holy war. When one person says something derogatory or anger based about another religious or spiritual belief the spirit of your words will feed the larger spirit of conflict and war that exists between and within religions and spiritual beliefs. This may sound odd to some but it is very true. As people argue and carry anger, hatred or rage towards another spiritual or religious belief we contribute to the spirit of a holy war. All we have to do to stop adding to the spirit of a holy war is to accept all the people that are in any and all religious and spiritual beliefs with no expectation that they change who they are or what they believe in. Acceptance is a very powerful force in creation. It has the power to transform darker more negative energies and spirit. Acceptance is a spiritual reality that naturally evolves in our collective spirit after we learn to create and manifest forgiveness and love. Therefore when people who have been at war with one another over spiritual and religious beliefs learn to forgive one another and them manifest a relationship based on love they will naturally learn to accept one another for who they are.

When the Roman Empire had been managing its empire for about 500 years they had a serious problem. All the tribes and nations under the 2,500,000 square miles of land mass that was the Roman Empire had their own belief in the god of their collective culture. The leaders of the empire knew that if they could get everyone to unite and have just one god – the god of the Roman Empire – this collective spirit could become a very powerful force. A leader of the Roman Empire named Diocletian formed Diocese all throughout the empire and assigned Bishops as Governors to manage the affairs of the diocese. Diocletian combined the lands of several tribes or nations into one diocese. There were many diocese throughout the Roman Empire. Then about 30 years later the Catholic Church was formed and was given its charter to build one united faith or belief in one god – The god of the Roman Empire. This is where the concept of an all-powerful god began. The church also had a charter from god the creator. This charter was to document and continue the evolution and understanding of God the Creator and how creation works through each and every one of us individually and collectively. To support the efforts of the church the Roman Empire gave a great deal of power to the church. As time went on the Roman Empire dissolved and the church was left to fend for its self.

When the Catholic Church first began it created a book (the Bible) that would contain all of the beliefs that currently existed all throughout the empire. This book is called the Roman Catholic Bible or more commonly named the King James Bible. This book and the rituals of the church have their beginnings in an effort to preserve the knowledge and understanding of all the beliefs that existed in the empire at that point in time. It was the best way to try to peacefully bring everyone together as one united faith in creation. After the empire failed the church was left with the book they created and the will of God the creator. Many people still had faith in and followed the guidance of the churches leaders but the church had to continue its quest for God the Creator while living in a world that contained quite a dark collective spirit at that point in time.

By now you should be able to see that God the Creator created creation. His creation is a place that allows all of us to live and exist while learning about ourselves and our power to create and to manifest. It was only natural that we would first manifest through our fears. It was these fears that disconnected us from or knowledge of creation thereby leaving us to manifest what we wanted, needed, desired and craved. We manifested the gods that came from our collective spirits. Now, today we are all growing collectively into a brighter light and learning to grow into a state of creation. As we allow creation to come through our thoughts words and actions we will grow into a higher consciousness. With a higher consciousness we will let the love and light of a brighter spirit and its consciousness guide our thoughts, words and actions. This is how to let God the Creator become a part of our lives. This is a reality of creation that exists through evolution. From generation to generation this process of creating a greater spirit and higher consciousness allows evolution to manifest a better way of life.

Many people today are becoming aware of the little bit of light that is in all of us; some refer to this as the spark of God or God's spark. My question to you is this:

What would you have if you were able to put together all of these little sparks into one great big collective spark?

You would have the God of the Living.

Those that live collectively with light in their spirit and love in their hearts would represent the God of the Living. Collectively, those that live with a spirit that is not capable of holding light (therefore exist in darkness and are not capable of creating through the light of God) would be the God of the dead.

What would you have if you were to put together all of these sparks that ever existed or lived?

This would be the entire collective spirit of mankind that lives life-time after life-time and generation after generation repeatedly changing the collective spirit of mankind (God).

Then of course there is God the Creator that created the heaven and the earth and awaits all of our return to glory someday when we have learned what we came here to learn about creation. When we have learned what we came here to learn we will have re-created our spirit and soul in such a way as to become one in God consciousness again.

Throughout this book you will learn how the Bible captured the essence of what many people today refer to as Source (the source of all emotion and consciousness) when it referred to the kingdom of the heavens. You will also learn that others refer to a Supreme Being or Great Mind and the Bible refers to this as the Son of Man (collective consciousness). The Son of Man is the collective Soul of Mankind and the Kingdom of the Heavens is the Source of all emotions and consciousness.

This book will explain to you how the individual and collective spirit of mankind exists in the kingdom of the heavens (Source) and creates through the collective soul of mankind (The Son of Man). The story that is explained through the images and symbols of the prophecy "The Revelation of Christ" explains the spirit and souls quest from the dark side of the heavens through the light and into the bright side of these heavens. The final phase of this quest is the transformation of the collective spirit and soul into the kingdom of God.

AN INTRODUCTION TO CREATION

Creation is all about the personal spirit we create through our intentions, emotions and the essence of who we are at the moment of creation. The moment of creation is that moment in time when the essence of our words, thoughts and actions combine with the emotion of our intention as the spirit of our creation becomes our personal spirit.

Creation is all about the spirit of that which we manifest through our thoughts, words and actions.

Creation is all about the reality we create because our personal spirit is either angry or loving when we manifest the spirit of our thoughts, words and actions. What we manifest will become our reality.

FEELINGS & EMOTIONS

Before learning the rules of creation you must first learn about emotions and feelings.

PLEASE REMEMBER

We feel feelings and we express emotions.

We are quite often motivated to act on our feelings. We combine an emotion with an intention and a spiritual creation will exist in our lives; in our spirit. It is the essence of our spirit at that moment in time when we express ourselves that will become the essence of that which we create.

Emotions and intentions are linked together in creation. You cannot have one without the other. A weak intention will generate a weak emotional commitment to that which you will create. While an intention that has a lot of commitment to it will generate a stronger emotional presence in that which you create. It is the commitment you have to your intention that will determine the strength and power of that which you create. Commitment will come through in your thoughts, words and actions as you strive to create a reality in your life.

INTENTION

Many people today believe they merely have to wake up every morning with an intention to love and then over time they will have done what they need to do to create love in their life. This is not completely true. They only manifest a less than pure spirit that surrounds them. This practice does not create a positive love-based personal spirit. Pure love is the love that will flow through you when your spirit is capable of holding light. Pure love will allow the love that flows from the heavens (the source of all emotions and consciousness) to become a part of your life.

When we try to express love through a spirit that is not capable of holding light the love is un-pure (some people will sense or feel this love as being a fake or false love). It is like wearing a mask of emotions that are not pure. This mask works in such a way as to allow a person to deny the anger within them while rationalizing that they have done the work they need to do to grow a spirit that will allow pure love to flow through them.

Quite often there is so much darkness in a person's spirit that he or she cannot express pure love. An example of how un-pure love is expressed is when someone enters a room, sees an old acquaintance and in a very loud voice says, "Oh my God, how long has it been since the last time we spoke – It must have been at least 5 years." A person manifests un-pure love in this way because he or she does not really mean what she is saying; the intention is insincere therefore the love is not pure. Many people will sense and feel this insincerity and think to themselves, "If you liked me so much then why has it been so long since we last spoke?" In this situation many people are not capable of allowing pure love to just flow through their spirit so they emote in such a way as to try to create something positive. This person will feel small or weak. A person with a weak spirit has to announce their presence by raising their voice. Their intention might not be to say hello to the other person but to let everyone else know they are entering the room. This un-pure intention has nothing to do with the other person or the words that are being spoken. When an intention is self-centered or self-serving but someone tries to use love to serve their need to be the center of attention the love that is expressed is not pure.

On the other hand when a person means what they say and truly wants to express a positive emotion they do not have to manifest it, they merely have to say what they mean and mean what they say. When your intention is pure the emotions that accompany them will be pure. When you have a spirit that is capable of holding light your love of life can just flow through you as you speak. When your body is capable of allowing love to flow through it, the spirit you create through your words is a reflection (or expression) of the pureness of your-self.

Love should flow through you not be something that you have to manifest. Many people are not capable of this level of love and this is OK. Just do the best you can with what you have.

THE ESSENCE OF YOUR CREATION

A person with a weak spirit is less capable of creating through his or her own personal essence. Each and every one of us has a personal essence; it is like a spiritual finger print. When a person's spirit is weak his or her essence is not strong enough to create through them. As a person's spirit is broken down the essence of this person becomes smaller and smaller until it is so small it cannot be recognized in your life. When a person's spirit and soul are broken into pieces there is a small part of your essence that goes with each small piece of the broken spirit and soul. Then as you heal from a broken spirit all these pieces come together as one being of love and light. After a spirit and soul heals it is stronger than it was before the hardships, trauma or abuse that hurt it in the first place.

When a person has a weak spirit the only spirit that he or she is capable of processing through their spirit is the darker spirit that comes from the kingdom of the heavens (the source of all emotions and consciousness). There are seven levels of darkness each having its own essence through which a weak spirit will create. As a person learns to re-create his or her spirit and soul the essence of the person becomes stronger. As the love and light grows in a person he or she becomes capable of love and light through his or her thoughts, words and actions. As the spiritual healing continues the essence of love and light will become a stronger part of your creations; this process of your spirit becoming stronger, your essence growing in your spirit and your ability to process love and light in your creations continues until your essence is strong enough to create on its own. When your essence is strong enough to create on its own you will no longer need the benefits of the kingdom of heaven (Source) to help you learn to create. As you become one in body, spirit and soul your essence is all that you will need to create the realties in your life and your existence.

THE PROCESS OF CREATION

The process of creation is quite simple, in theory. The essence, intention and emotion of everything we say think and do, creates our personal spirit and manifests the spirit of our thoughts, words and actions which will become the reality that is our lives.

The spirit of our thoughts, words and actions is made up of the intention and the emotions that we are feeling at this moment of creation. The essence of that which is created is a function of either the essence of the spirit of creation or your personal essence. We create through anger-based emotions and the essence of anger, hatred or rage when our spirit is not capable of holding light. When our spirit is capable of holding light we create and manifest through love.

An intention can be either positive or negative. When a person has a positive intention his or her spirit fills with the intention. Like a cup is filled with water – a person's spirit can be half full or it can overflow. A person's commitment to his or her intention will determine how full his spirit will become. As a person speaks, the spirit of his words will be a function of the commitment to this intention. If an intention has a greedy nature to it then the essence of greed will become part of this creation. Greed has its essence in wants and needs

– A very needy person will strive to have more than he or she needs. Some needy people have an intention to take what they want or need from someone else. To take from others has a direct impact on your personal spirit. It creates a greater sense of neediness. It also creates greed in the ambient spirit of mankind (that which we manifest collectively). Greed has a natural emotion associated with it – this emotion is usually based in anger. When a person breaks up with a significant other he or she might feel anger towards the other person and a shopping spree might be in needed to make this feeling of anger go away. This is when a person creates through the essence of greed.

THE KINGDOM OF THE HEAVENS - THE SOURCE OF ALL EMOTIONS, THOUGHTS, AWARENESS AND CONSCIOUSNESS

The source of all emotions and consciousness (the kingdom of the heavens) has two sides to it – light and dark. Each side has seven parts within it. These seven parts are: dark has wrath, greed, lust, gluttony, sloth, pride or envy; light has love of God, nature and creation, Love of self, love of others, compassion (which is love for those that wish you harm), a passion for creation, a passion for making the world a better place, just being and letting the world be what it will be.

The essence of greed is the <u>wants and needs</u> that motivate us to act when we want or need to feel good but for some reason cannot just feel good. Greed will involve using things to make you feel good.

The essence of lust is the <u>desires</u> that motivate us to act when we use people to make us feel good about our-self.

The essence of gluttony is the <u>cravings</u> that motivate us to act when we are consumed by the need to use things and/or people to feel good about life in general.

The essence of sloth is the <u>blahs that de-motivate us</u>; they create a state of mind that is totally lacking in a desire to do anything. We do not feel good and just do not care anymore.

The essence of pride is the <u>sense of self-centeredness</u> that motivates us to act without feelings or concern for others. The spirit of pride encourages us to live for our-selves and only for those that we feel we are responsible for. As if it is our duty or responsibility to take care of someone like parents, and family. With the spirit of pride at our side we strive to survive. In this state of mind the only things that makes us happy is a sense of knowing that we have done the best we can with what we have. People that are filled with a sense of pride gain comfort in knowing they are doing at least a little bit better than they perceive others are doing – given the same circumstances that they perceive exist around them.

The essence of envy is an <u>all-consuming desire to have what makes others happy</u> or prevent others from having what they need to be happy. The old adage, "misery loves company" is the best way to describe this state of mind.

When a person lives their life in one of these darker states of mind it is like being consumed by the spirit of greed, lust etc....

THE REALITY OF LIFE

The only true reality in life is change. Change is inevitable; life is about how we resist change or embrace it. While resistance is futile, it is also a reality that exists within each of us. Change is THE REALITY AND THE INTENTION of God's creation.

What happens is this – when people have hardships in their lives their spirit breaks. A broken spirit then loses its ability to love and eventually the ability to forgive those that created these hurtful experiences. Without forgiveness in your spirit you become sealed away from the light side of the heavens. At this point you lose the spirit that used to fill your heart with love. When you no longer feel good about your-self you strive to use things and people to feel good. As you act on or through the essence of the wants and needs, desires and cravings of these darker spirits, you create your own spirit through the essence of greed, lust, gluttony etc.... When your spirit is filled with greed, lust, gluttony et al. your thoughts and feelings motivate you to act; then you manifest through emotions that are a reflection of these feelings. As you create through the essence of these older motivators you create more of that which has existed for thousands of years. In a sense, we feed off of these age old spirits and when we react to feelings that come from them; we feed them.

The foundation for these anger-based states of mind is fear. Fear is a very important feeling to live and exist with. Many if not all people are taught to deny that they feel fear. There have been great phrases that have helped us to learn to live without fear for many generations; phrases like, "feel the fear and do it anyways" or the old mocking phrase, "What, are you afraid?" There is no wisdom in these phrases. For many people, the result of hearing these phrases is to learn to deny or ignore the feeling of fear. Fear, like any other feeling carries with it information; it is trying to tell us something. Quite often it is trying to tell us to not listen to those people that are teaching us to deny the fear we are feeling.

When a person walks into the room and I feel fear I know that there is something about that person I should be aware of; I try to either avoid or gain a better understanding of this person.

When a person walks in the door and I feel a sense of comfort from him or her that tells me something completely different. With this person I learn to feel comfortable working with him or her.

When a person encourages me to deny feeling fear I always question his or her intention. They usually have a private agenda for what they are saying or doing. Usually they are trying to help someone become just like themselves.

For thousands of years, the essence of these motivators that motivate us to create have come from a darker base. We have created a spiritual foundation that is based on greed, lust gluttony, sloth, pride and envy. Currently we have just begun to create through a spirit that is not as dark; we are beginning to be able to create light. This has a big impact on the current younger generations. Since past generations have created a world that was based on creating through the spirit of pride with its motivations; these younger generations have no base or foundation on which to create the love and light they are meant to build. As time goes on – life time after life time and generation after generation this new foundation will be built; but until then we are going to experience a lot of confusion and turmoil in the spirit that exists between generations. These younger generations will re-create the collective spirit of mankind and the manifested spirit of the world. This is the spiritual generation gap.

AN EXAMPLE OF CREATING THROUGH GLUTTONY:

When a person feels an overwhelming need, desire or craving to do something there is usually no love involved. There is usually a strong negative reality in his or her life and they just feel consumed by some negative feeling like deep anger, sadness, worry etc.… In this state of mind a person tries to do something that will make the negative or darker feelings they are experiencing at that moment, go away. The intention is to make them-selves feel better and this leads to an action that will process these negative feelings through a person's thoughts, words and actions. Acting on these feelings will create a spirit with an intent to get rid of these negative feelings or to share them with others. It is the sense of being consumed by these feelings that identifies the gluttonous state a person is in. When some people are consumed by life's traumas and tragedies they will turn to drugs, alcohol, sex or other addictive behaviors in order to not feel the darkness of other personal spirit. Some people try to hurt others so they do not have to feel the darkness of the reality they live in.

AN EXAMPLE OF HOW A PERSON CREATES HIS OR HER OWN SPIRIT AND THEN SHARES THAT SPIRIT WITH OTHERS – HOW THE COLLECTIVE SPIORIT OF MANKIND WORKS

When a woman lives with the suffering that comes with losing the light of her personal spirit she will naturally feel the darkness of her spirit. If the darkness of her spirit was created by doing hurtful things to others she may feel ugly inside. This is the ugliness of the spirit she created for herself. Naturally she will not want to feel this way all the time and will strive to give that feeling away to someone else. When she finds someone that she is jealous of, she will naturally try to make the person that she is jealous of feel bad. Jealousy will consume your spirit very quickly. By directing her feelings of ugliness at the other person she will be able to give it away as she attempts to make the other person feel ugly. The other person may not have done anything wrong and may not deserve this spiritual attack. If her spiritual strength is not strong enough to prevent this jealous person from asserting her will in to her spirit she will then feel ugly and then act on her feelings. This is how people with a darker spirit exist all throughout their lives. It is only natural that a person with a darker spirit will say negative things about other people; either behind their back or just to insult them directly while talking to them. Insults and back stabbing are opposite sides of the same coin.

In order to facilitate the re-creation of a spirit that has existed for thousands of years we have to learn to live by a set of spiritual rules. There are ten rules that need to be followed as we re-create our personal spirit, the collective spirit of mankind and the ambient spirit of the world.

WHY IS THE COLLECTIVE SPIRIT AND SOUL SO IMPORTANT TO EACH AND EVERYONE OF US

Many people today talk about the collective spirit and collective consciousness but:

What is it? How does it work? Why is it so important to all of us?

Many people today talk about the spark within each and every one of us. They often refer to it as the God spark or spark of God. People then talk about how God is in us and that this spark is a part of God.

My question to you is this – If you took all of those little tiny sparks that exist in each of us and put them all together what would you have?

Answer:

You would have the collective spirit and soul of mankind. In one sense you will have God. When all of mankind is ready to accept the reality that collectively we are God (not the creator) and we collectively create the spirit of God on earth, we will have achieved the "WE ARE US" Consciousness.

There is the God that is the collective spirit and soul of mankind and then there is God the Creator. In the parables of the Bible Jesus refers to this collective spirit and soul of mankind as "The Son of Man". In the prophecy "The Revelations of Christ" the collective spirit and soul is represented as, "The Son of Man Walking among Seven Candlesticks and Seven Churches". Spiritual beliefs refer to this collective soul as the "Supreme Being". In the Catholic Bible there are several references to God – God the Father, The Living God, The God of the Living, the God of the Dead and the God of Jacob and Isaac and Abraham.

God the Father is the Creator who created the heavens (the source of all feelings, emotions and consciousness).

The Living God is the ambient spirit that exists all around the world. We create this ambient spirit and it lives on from generation to generation. It changes as each generation brings its own love and light into the world.

The God of the Dead is the spirit that exists within the collective spirit of mankind and is dead to creation. This is the part of the collective spirit that is not capable of holding light therefore it is dark or dead to creation.

The God of the Living is the spirit that exists in the collective spirit of mankind and is alive to creation. This is the part of the collective spirit that is capable of holding light therefore it is alive and living in creation.

The God of Jacob and Isaac and Abraham is the collective spirit of the family that started when Abraham was alive. The family was then led by Isaac and finally by Jacob. As the story goes Jacob tricked his father into giving him the blessing instead of his twin brother Esau. This blessing made him the head of the family, after his father (Isaac) died. After stealing the blessing from his brother, Jacob left the family for many years. He lived with his uncle and married two women both daughters of his uncle. When he returned home to his family more than a decade later he sent his wives and children ahead of him to meet with his family. That night he stayed alone in the desert. During the night he wrestled with (some Bibles say he fought with) God and won. He then took the name Israel and the family of Abraham was then referred to as Israel.

How can someone fight with God and win? Only if he wrestled with his conscience and the collective spirit of the family he betrayed and the memories of the things he did to his brother, father and others.

When he wrestled with his conscience and won he learned to accept responsibility for his actions, he repented (sought forgiveness) for what he had done and successfully transformed his spirit into a light based spirit and soul. When the polarity of a person's spirit changes the old spirit is gone and new reality begins for the person. This is why his name was then changed to Israel. When a spirit transforms itself completely it will have a different feel to it and this is why it should receive a new name. This different feeling comes from his spirit's polarity changing from dark to light.

THE COLLECTIVE SPIRIT

The collective spirit is important because it represents that which we are all capable of living within. The range and depth of feelings that we are capable of receiving are determined by the capacity of the collective spirit to feel. There is the kingdom of the heavens that feed us feelings, emotions and consciousness. The kingdom of the heavens is the total capacity that exists; but mankind has only explored a portion of this source of all feelings. We are limited in what we can experience through our feelings by the collective spirit's evolution into these heavens. As we continue to lift the veil of darkness that exists in the collective spirit we will continue to experience a greater light in our spirit and feel more love in our hearts. This interaction between the heavens and our collective spirit is very important to understand. The heavens are the potential to feel while the collective spirit sets the range of feelings and emotions we can experience. Then our personal range of feelings and emotions are limited by our commitment to the spirit of the collective. When someone overcomes the comfort of the collective spirit and ventures beyond it, he or she will create a path for others to follow.

If a feeling does not exist within the collective spirit then someone has to live his of her life in such a way as to grow their individual spirit to a level that is beyond or outside of the collective. Jesus grew beyond the range of the collective spirit and lived with a higher vibration (that came from the kingdom of the heavens) than anyone else at that point in time. This is how Jesus created forgiveness in the collective spirit of mankind. When he said the Son of Man will forgive you, he was saying that he had fulfilled his purpose which was to create forgiveness within the collective spirit and soul of mankind. From the time of his death forward, forgiveness would be available so we would be able to create it within our own personal spirits.

THE COLLECTIVE CONSCIOUSNESS

The collective soul is important because it is where the collective consciousness (the collective right and wrong) comes from. This is not the same as knowing that it is wrong to lie, steal or date your friend's spouse. The collective consciousness feeds us the rationalization that comes with the reality you create when you are not telling the truth, stealing or dating your friend's spouse. This rationalization and the feeling that it is acceptable to do something that you know is inherently wrong come from the collective consciousness. The collective consciousness feeds us thoughts that encourage a particular behavior based on the norms established by society (the soul of society is the collective consciousness). When a person grows his spirit into a lighter state of mind the conscious awareness he or she lives with, comes from the collective and the collective draws its knowledge and awareness from the light side of the heavens. This source of consciousness feeds the collective consciousness and then you will be able to follow the same path into light as those that went before you. When a person walks his own path and does not follow the path created by the collective he or she will endure a more difficult learning process and will pave a new path for others to follow. It is more difficult because the feelings and thoughts you experience will be different from others. This means that others can't help you along the way and you will not feel like you fit in with others. When growing beyond the collective it will not be as important to feel like you fit in. When you are in a higher light you are very comfortable just being you although, from time to time, you might wish you could just fit in again. It is a learning process that everyone experiences over time. The collective spirit and the feelings that accompany it will determine the knowledge, awareness and thoughts that come into the collective consciousness.

The collective consciousness is also the knowledge that comes with being committed to a purpose in your life. When your spirit grows into a higher vibration you will naturally feel compelled to have a greater purpose in your life. How to accomplish this purpose is a function of your commitment to this purpose and the light in your spirit. As your desire to help others (which can be everyone in the world, the collective spirit and soul) you can and will receive what you <u>need to know</u> in order to make the impact you desire. What you need to know is knowledge that comes from the heavens (Source). This knowledge comes through the needs of the collective spirit and soul to you. Your deep rooted feelings and intention to help creates the spirit of your intention. The spirit of your intention opens the door to this source of knowledge and then comes up through the spirit of your intentions; then what you need to know enters your consciousness. When you let yourself learn in this fashion you will know what you need to know; then as you do what has to be done to change your reality (more information and knowledge) will then enter your consciousness. This is how people continue to make this world a better place.

THE COLLECTIVE SPIRIT AND SOUL (CONSCIOUSNESS)

Thousands of years ago, the collective consciousness and collective spirit had 5 layers within them.

1) The sex you are born into – male or Female
2) The family you are born into
3) The tribe you live in
4) The nation or you are a part of
5) The entire world which is the connection between all nations and tribes

Today, we all live and exist within part of the collective spirit of others that do similar things as we do. These other people are people that are of the same spirit as we are; they are like-minded people. It is like a room in the collective mind where everyone with similar spirits lives and exists. The people in this like-mind strive to create a world that will allow their spirit and soul to exist. There are two sides to each of the sections of the collective spirit; one side that strives to survive (survives in dark) and one side that lives with a sense of purpose (thrives in light). The following is a list of examples of how this reality might exist in your life.

1) Politicians live in either; the spirit of politics and their own individual power, influence and control or in the spirit of doing what is truly best for the people of their nation?
2) Athletes live in either; in the spirit of surviving so they can keep their position on the team or the spirit of sports?
3) Teachers live in either; the spirit of educating students or the spirit of the teachers union?
4) Autoworkers live in either; the spirit of making the best possible car for the people that drive them or the spirit of the unions that allow them to keep their job?

How do you live your life?

With a sense of purpose in everything you do or do you play it safe and strive to survive?

How you live your life may be different in every situation and every situation changes day-to-day. How many different ways does your spirit change throughout one day? Make a list throughout your day.

Today a majority of the aspects of the collective spirit exist in the spirit of money and finance. The spirit of business, money and finance is what we (all the people of the world) have been creating for more than 2,000 years. Working together all around the world to make a living for ourselves is a good thing. Working together in a world that is centered on maintaining what we have and improving our way of life is a great thing. It is something that we have done and continue to do together; collectively. There is nothing wrong with this; although, what we should do is look closely at the spirit of greed that has manifested within our day to day lives as we have worked to survive. The spirit of greed within it is what we all have to learn to overcome as we expand our collective spirit and soul into a higher light. This can be done by simply living to be grateful and generous in everything we say, think and do.

It is important to restate that 2,000 years ago the collective spirit of the world was structured around individual people (and the gender), the languages of different people, their tribes and nations. Today the collective spirit of the world has changed and is defined both vertically by families, communities (tribes) and nations as well as horizontally by how we work to fund the lifestyle we live. The structure of the collective spirit is rotating from a vertical top down structure that was control centered into a horizontal structure that will allow everyone to be connected and to grow throughout our lives as we live to make this world a better place. The key to successfully navigating in this collective is to work together towards a common goal. Perhaps this why so many people all around the world are trying to make changes that will remove the barriers that made the old structures work. As pride leaves our collective spirit we will have to find something else to motivate us to work – perhaps this will be a love of nature, or perhaps a love for one another. Eventually money will be seen as the last barrier that will need to be changed. As people work to be happy not for the money they need to make themselves happy; greed will leave the spirit of mankind and the need for money will simply leave our reality.

Our collective spirit grows and changes from generation to generation. The current collective exists as the result of about 3 ½ generations of people that lived during a 75 year period of time. These generations re-create the world and transform it into what it is at any point in time. Then a new generation comes into the world with the purpose to change the foundation of that which had been created by the previous generations. There are three generations whose purposes are linked to one another to continue to make this world a better place. The first of the three generations changes the spirit of the collective spirit and soul; the second generation continues with these changes by letting the spiritual changes that began, grow into a new consciousness; with a higher vibrating spirit and a consciousness driven by a new purpose, the third generation changes the realities within the world making it a better place. The ½ generation puts closure to the changes that were made and prepares for the next set of changes that come from our desire to make to make the world a better place for your grandchildren. Prayers and desires of people from previous generations come together to form the spirit of the purpose of the next set of changes that will enter the world.

The spirit of children coming into the world are consumed by the spirit of the collective that exists and their desires to make the world a better place. These two realities combine to create the spirit of the next three generations.

When a new generation enters the world they bring their higher love and light as well as a purpose to change the world. What they need to know in order to make these changes comes from their collective spirit and consciousness.

Human nature is a function of the collective spirit and consciousness. Human nature is that which a large group of people sense, feel and know are right or wrong. It is only natural for human nature to change with each and every generation. This is what we call the generation gap. A generation gap is the difference in behavioral norms that exists between generations.

This gap is getting bigger and growing faster with each and every generation. This is because we are collectively entering the light side of the heavens. As we continue to grow the collective spirit and soul into this lighter and soon to be brighter state of being we will find a greater peace of mind that will lead to peace on earth.

Over time the generation gap will slow down because peace will feel like the norm and this will bring with it a sense of calmness and acceptance. As acceptance enters our collective spirit and soul, competition will leave it. As acceptance grows the desire to change the world into something better will fade away as we accept that it is already good enough. This is when we will have reached a milestone collectively; we will be more accepting of change while at the same time not need to make change happen. This dichotomy is what acceptance is all about.

CREATING THROUGH THE COLLECTIVE SPIRIT AND SOUL

When you create through God's creation(s) you can and will change your reality in life.

You allow a new reality to impact your life by allowing creation to work through you. To do this you allow the intentions and feelings that lie within you to create through your thoughts words and actions. Who you are and what your true intentions and feelings are will always come through your thoughts, words and actions. No matter how much you try to mask your intentions and feelings about someone or something they will <u>naturally</u> create through you. They will create the spirit of you at that moment of creation. This is nature's way. When your internal (or natural) intentions and your desired intentions are in alignment you will have found your-self. From this point in time forward you will have a desire to live with a purpose that truly comes from within. There will be no desire to manifest things or money into your life. There will be no need for things. All you will want to do is what makes you happy, what makes you feel good. This is when creation enters your life and your purpose fills your spirit and soul naturally.

THE DIFFERENCE BETWEEN MANIFESTATION AND CREATION – A MASK OF DECEPTION

When people do not walk their talk they manifest a mask of deception. When people carry anger in their spirit and try to cover it up by trying to do a lot of things to convince others that they do not have all that anger they manifest their mask. Many people can present their mask to people they meet infrequently and these people will assume this person has a positive love-based reality. Then after getting to know this person at a deeper level they find this person is not all that loving but only wearing a mask that is now revealed. People that wear masks of deception have to do something good for others and then have to tell everyone they did it. They usually exaggerate what they did. In many cases someone else does most of the work while a person wearing a mask takes credit for the efforts of others. This is how they manifest this mask of deception. This too is a very natural thing for people to do. For people that wear a mask it is not about the charitable act; it is about the attention they get after doing it. As they talk about how good they are they manifest this spiritual mask. After they create this mask they have to maintain it. Maintaining this mask is about being involved with others that do charitable deeds so they can tell more people about what they did.

To manifest is to attempt to make your reality what you want it to be, while creation is allowing your reality to just be what it is and to accept it as it is. When you just allow yourself to be and to accept the good, the bad and the ugly that is your life, you become more aware of who, you are. When you accept you for who you are, not who you want to be or who you want others to think you are, you can then assess the good and bad things you did in your life. You have to accept the bad as bad before you can truly deal with it. This is when creation can work through you.

Creation does not create the love you manifest:

1) When you deny that you have done anything wrong and only want to accept that part of your life that you think was good.
2) When you rationalize that the bad things you did were acceptable.

Creation will manifest that which you are not that which you want to be or that which you try to convince others that you are.

The power of creation comes from aligning your true self and your intentions with your thoughts, words and actions. This alignment brings your essence, spirit and soul through you with every thought, word and action, instead of trying to deny who you are and then manifest through this mask or false face. When you have this power to create, you can then create what you need in order to accomplish your purpose in life not manifest your wants and needs. Creation is a system that contains a set of processes that work through you and me naturally to recreate our spirits and souls (individually and collectively). This is how a person manifests his or her personal spirit. Manifestation is also the assertion of your personal will power to manifest something in your life; it is the use of the spirit of nature to make something happen that you want, need, desire or crave.

Advantages and Disadvantages of Manifestation

Advantages:

1) When you manifest a more positive spirit around you - It helps you to live with anger and not feel as bad as you would if you did not manifest a more positive spirit around you.

2) When you manifest things in your life - It helps you survive with the things you want and need so you will feel better while you continue to live in an anger-based reality.

3) When many people strive to manifest the same things in their lives they are combining an intention and a deep rooted desire to make their life better. Collectively we may not be able to create happiness in our spirit and soul but that deep rooted desire and intention will feed the spirit and soul of future generations that will then come into the world more prepared to create happiness.

Disadvantages:

1) You will not create true happiness that will be a part of your life

2) You will still feel the need to have things and to use people to make you happy

3) You continue to deny your spirit's darkness and your true self. Denial of your true self is like leaving your spirit and soul to fend for its-self while you convince your-self that you are someone (something) that you are not. This is why it is so important to recognize when you are rationalizing. Rationalization can be a very deadly thing to do to your soul.

THE TWELVE RULES OF CREATION

STOP CREATING AND PERPETUATING THE DARKER SPIRITS OF THE WORLD
STOP CREATING THROUGH THESE DARKER SPIRITS

Rule #1 – Anger - Identify it; always work to eliminate it from your life.

Rule #2 – Lust – First learn the full range of experiences in your life that attach you to the spirit of lust. Then work to eliminate lust from your life. Even lustful thoughts create more lust in your life. Using, manipulating and deceiving others are forms of lust.

Rule #3 – Don't make promises to God – Just do it – Create your reality in life.

Rule #4 – Revenge - Don't volley someone else's anger.

Rule #5 –Love completely - Especially those that wish you harm

BEGIN CREATING THE LOVE BASED SPIRIT THAT WILL BE THE FOUNDATION OF THE SPIRIT THAT WILL PROPEL US INTO THE FUTURE

Rule #6 – Do not be afraid to cry or mourn a loss. Trying to put on a happy face so others will think you are strong when faced with sorrow will only prevent you from creating your personal spirit to be as healthy as it can be.

Rule #7 – Forgive, Forgive, Forgive – Forgive others, forgive your-self and then forgive again

Rule #8 – Love deeply in everything you say, think and do.

Rule #9 - Be righteous – Always strive to just do the right thing. Live with an intention to always do what you know to be the right thing to do.

Rule #10 – Give generously and be grateful as often as you possibly can.

Rule #11 – Share the love you feel throughout your life with everyone you meet. When you share your love with others – do it with purpose.

Rule #12 - Be purposeful in everything you do in life make sharing love a part of your purpose in life. To be purposeful and to be as positive as you can be in your life will make your purpose stronger.

In simple terms the best way to grow through these processes, rules and realities is simply to:
Live, Love and Laugh. Then be led by your inner voice as you receive more positive thoughts.

RULE #1 - ANGER

QUESTIONS AND TIPS TO THINK ABOUT AS YOU READ RULE #1

How often do you experience anger?

Do you experience anger every day or every hour of every day?

What level of anger do you experience anger, hatred, rage?

Do you sometimes feel a total lack of desire to care about someone?

Do you sometimes feel a total lack of desire to care about anyone?

How do you react to these feelings?

Do you act on them? Do you try to make them go away?
If yes, what do you do to make them go away?

Do you ignore them?

Do you try to deny they exist?

Do you take them out on someone? If yes, who?

Is it the person you are truly mad at or someone else that maybe represents the person you are actually mad at?

Are you the person you are mad at?

To learn more about where your anger comes from - ask yourself why are you angry?

Write down your answer. Then reread it.

Now, ask your-self why are you angry, who are you angry at and what are you angry about? Write down your answer. Then reread it. And continue to the next step.

Again, ask your-self why are you angry, who are you angry at and what are you angry about?

Write down your answer. Then reread it. And continue to the next step.

Ask yourself these questions again and write down your answers. Then reread it and continue to the next step.

Continue this process of asking why 5 times and when you are done you should have a new awareness as to where your anger comes from.

RULE #1 - ANGER

Always strive to identify anger and eliminate it from your life.
Always strive to understand where and why anger exists in your life.

Try to learn the source of the anger?
   How does this anger manifest in your spirit (perhaps from an experience in your past) and why does someone or something trigger it?

Forgive those that hurt you in the past.
Always forgive those that continue to do hurtful things to you.

THE REALITY OF ANGER

Anger is an important reality in creation. When we create through anger we add the spirit of anger to the spirit we create through our thoughts, words and actions.

Anger is the lowest level of the spirit of wrath. Anger grows into hatred and hatred grows into rage. When a person lives with any of these levels of anger they create more of that which they are and this is something we all strive to improve in our lives.

Anger is associated with things that go wrong in our day-to-day lives.
Hatred is associated with people that we do not like throughout our day-to-day lives.
Rage is the highest level of anger that we express when we are consumed by things that go wrong and people that upset us in our day-to-day lives.

WHERE DOES ANGER COME FROM

Many people believe that we own all of our feelings as if they are something that we control or something that we cannot control. Many people think that feelings are just there and we accept them as we feel them. This is not the whole story about feelings and emotions though.

The first reality we need to accept about feelings and emotions, is that we feel or receive feelings and we express emotions. It is natural to feel a feeling and then emit the same as an emotion. As we learn to understand our feelings and emotions we can learn to consciously accept a feeling that is positive and reject those that are negative. Simply by learning to recognize what we are receiving and to accept the realities that we can choose to accept what comes to us or reject it. We do not have to act on every feeling that we receive – we choose to accept a feeling simply by acting on it. When we act on it with intention we are allowing it to create through us. Please learn to allow only good feelings to flow through you and only allow yourself to have positive intentions when any feeling creates through you.

ANGER CAN COME FROM WITHIN YOU.

Anger can come from issues that started in your life when you were younger. Unresolved issues are the doorway to the anger that existed during the experience that caused the issue. Anger can come from issues that started in a past life.

ANGER CAN COME FROM A SOURCE THAT IS OUTSIDE OF YOU

Anger can come from others that you interact with on a day to day basis. You can become infected by someone else's feelings. This is more prevalent in small or large groups that we associated with. For example the spirit of a family, workplace or school, or classroom can impact our personal spirit. By simply going to work every day we become a part of the collective spirit of our workplace.

Anger can come from the air around you – this is called the ambient spirit of the world. For thousands of years people have been living and creating through negative intentions; their thoughts, words and actions have created some of the darkest spirits this world has ever seen. More recently, we have also created through some of the strongest positive intentions this world has ever seen.

Anger can come from the collective spirit of mankind. The collective spirit of mankind is the collective spirit of people that connects all of us as one. This is that feeling that makes us feel as if it is OK to do something because everyone else is doing it. This is something we rationalize that it is normal and acceptable for us to do it. Our collective spirit connects us all as one. As a person stretches his or her personal spirit and its ability to love beyond the limits of the collective spirit, we begin to grow the collective spirit into a new and greater light. Please help all of us and strive to live and create at the deepest level of love and light possible. The collective spirit of mankind can make us feel as if it is ok to judge others or to think highly of others as long as they meet certain criteria. For example is a person works hard and is successful we might think highly of this person but a person who is just as successful but does not work as hard to get there can be judged as being not as good simply because he does not work hard enough. There are many realities that develop because of the collective spirit of mankind.

RULE #2 - LOVE

QUESTIONS AND TIPS TO THINK ABOUT AS YOU READ RULE #2

What is love?

Who do you love?

Who do you not love and why?

What is compassion?

Have you ever lost your ability to love someone?

Do you have a compulsive nature about you?

A compulsive nature is when you just do things because you get a feeling that motivates you to do something and then you just do it. If you try to stop this behavior or to not act on these feelings and it is a real struggle to stop – you have a compulsive nature about you. Some people are compulsive about sports and competition; others might not be able to stop themselves from going on a shopping spree.

ABOUT YOUR RELATIONSHIPS WITH OTHERS

Think about this very seriously – if it helps you, make a list of these items. These questions and your answers are designed to help you gain a more accurate understanding of you, how you live your life and who you really are without the rationalization that typically goes on inside your head. Rationalizing is how your mind tricks you into believing that you are in a much better state of mind than you actually are.

How do you express your love for yourself or for others?

Do you hope that someone will do something romantic for you or do you try to do something romantic for someone else?

Does sex make you feel better when you have a bad day at work or are carrying a lot of stress throughout your day?

Can you live without sex?
   Does sex motivate you to do things that you might later regret?

What feelings motivate you to take action?

   Do they manifest through anger or the suppression of anger?
   Do you express your anger or do you suppress and deny it?

Do you think it takes a lot to get you do things or to take action when needed or are you always on the go?

When you ever drive past a car accident when someone needs help:
Do you stop to help or just drive past?

If you drive past – a few hours or days later do you stop and think that maybe you should have stopped?

Do you usually go shopping or out with friends when these feelings enter your life? Where do you go shopping? Do you go to a restaurant of bar? What do you buy or who do you go to see?

Does it make you feel good to do something for someone else or for yourself?

Do you feed off of the need to feel good by doing something for someone else?

If you answered yes to either of the above 2 questions; you are using people to make yourself feel good. Much like most people today we try to feel good by making others feel good. This is because when we feel bad we do something to make us feel good. This is how the collective spirit works in a darker state of spirit; we feed off of each other's spirit in order to make us feel good.

After a person learns to get past the issues in their life he or she will no longer need to feed off of other people or things to feel good.

RULE #2 – LOVE, SEX, LUST AND CREATION

Today entire generations of people are trying to figure out what love is.

What is love to you?

Ask your friends what is love to them? Do not tell them what it means to you – truly listen to what they say it is and do not try to compare what they say it is to what you think love is. Just accept there concept of love as what they need to feel love is in the reality of their life. You will find it is a very different reality for almost everyone while at the same time you can probably group them together in different categories – Romantic love, physical, family love, self-love, emotional love, et al.

Try to define, what "healthy love" is to you (or what makes you feel good or comfortable in a relationship, thereby accepting a feeling as love)?

Is it having someone that is there to talk to you and to tell you they love you?

How often do you need to hear the words, "I love you"?

Do you say "I love you" because it makes you feel good to say it and then to hear it?

Does it become something you need to hear as if you have to feed off it?

Do you struggle to say the words, "I love you"?

Do you struggle to feel deep emotions?

This is how we use others to make us feel good about our-selves. When we need to hear it or to feed off of a relationship, we have a manifested love. Later in this book you will learn that these behaviors exist when our spirit is at a lower level called lust. This is how we use others to make us feel good about ourselves when we lose our love of self.

To need to hear these words in order to feel better about yourself or to feel secure in your relationship is a sign of a weaker spirit. To over love is a reflection of the same unhealthy personal spirit as to under love. Both are opposite sides of the same coin. It is the need to feed off of someone else that is the same as not being able to feed love to someone at all. It is the idea that we have to give all our love to someone in order to feel secure in a relationship that is a sign that things could be better. We should share our love but not give it away.

When your spirit is healthy you will just feel good without the need to receive anything from any one while at the same time feeling deeply about life in general.

MANIPULATION AND DECEPTION ARE REALITIES THAT COME FROM THE SPIRIT OF LUST

Manipulation – Using words and actions to convince someone to do something they ordinarily would not do. This is manipulating someone to get something you want, need or desire.

Deception – Using words to twist or manage a person's perception of what you are trying to tell them is the foundation of deception. People do this in an effort to use someone in such a way as to force someone to make the decision they want them to make. Quite often, they filter information instead of just giving someone the information that is needed to make an informed decision on their own.

The spirit of manipulation and deception goes back many life times. Both men and women use manipulation is different ways. For example, for many generations' people survived with very little and for the most part it was men that controlled what the family would have or would not have. This forced women to manipulate men into giving them what they wanted or needed. Another example is, when men had to make the best deals they could when buying things for their home. There were many people selling things that just were not what they seemed to be and people had to beware of these salesmen. This is where the phrase, "buyer beware" started. Once people relied on these behaviors to survive the spirit of their behaviors became a reality in everyone's life. The spirit of manipulation and deception still exist today; but it has taken on a different form. Today men and women manipulate and deceive each other on a regular basis; many call it dating. Women try to get men to change or to buy them things and men want to convince women to have sex with them.

HOW MEN AND WOMEN MANIPULATE EACH OTHER IN A RELATIONSHIP

MEN
Do you justify things that happen in a relationship because you told her something that she agreed too like, "making sure she knows you have no plans on getting married"?

When a woman starts talking about marriage, men know they are looking for a commitment. But they rationalize that it is ok to continue the relationship. Even though they know their girlfriend wants a commitment they rationalize that everything is OK because they told her they do not plan on making a commitment at that level. Many women then try to rationalize that they will eventually get him to change his mind thereby staying in the relationship as they both continue to do this dance of manipulation.

WOMEN

Do you ask a man questions about commitment on the first few dates so you can justify his commitment before having sex with him?
Does it really matter what his answer is?

For many women if they are going to have sex with a man it does not matter how he answers the questions. If you are not going to have sex with him it does not matter how he answers the questions; you are not going to have sex with him. For many people these questions are there just for the sake of rationalizing that it is acceptable to take that next step in the relationship. The problem most people face is that it feels right and these rationalizing thoughts tell us that everything is OK even though we do know there is something wrong with this situation. As one person in the relationship wants a commitment and the other does not, is when the dance of manipulation becomes a challenge for true manipulators as they build a relationship on trying to get something the other person does not want to give.

This is how we manipulate others in order to deceive our-self into proceeding in a relationship that, in our heart, we really know is not right for either person.

Manipulation and deception is the essence of the spirit of lust. Lust is a reality that exists in a person's life when the hardships he or she experienced created the loss of love of self.

Do you strive for a relationship where he says he loves you first?

You may not have to talk him into saying he loves you but if it is that important to you, it is in your spirit and he could very well say, "I love you" because it was in your Will that he do so. One of the most difficult realities to understand is that we need something so deep in our heart that it is in our spirit. When it is directed into our spirit the other person feels as if it is directed at him like cupids arrow was shot into his heart. Others will react to what is in our heart because it is also in our spirit. Quite often they feel and act on your needs and desires instead of their own personal feelings. This is how the collective spirit works and how the spirit of small groups and organizations work.

If you are now saying "then what do I have to do to get him to say I love you"; you should now ask yourself, "why is it so important to you that he say these words"? Why do you need to hear them?

Do you try to change the person you are with so he or she will become the person you want them to be; the person you need them to be?

Do you try to make sure these changes are small and you always give him some kind of reward like a smile or a touch or the kind of sex he likes; so he will like you and then return to you and give you the feelings that you need and desire?

Perhaps you are trying to change others instead of changing your-self.

How often do you recognize a personal opportunity to develop your-self spiritually?

SEX AND LUST

Do you believe that he will respect you in the morning because you wait until a certain number of dates go by 2, 3 or maybe 4 before you sleep with him? Does he have to say or do something so you can feel as if it is right to take that next step in your relationship?

Face it – you know that respect and intimacy have nothing to do with one another- But perhaps it is a social norm that your friends created to make themselves feel as if it is OK to have sex with someone as long as it is on their terms. Social norms are realities that a group of people establish as values and realities that determine what is right and wrong. As social groups establish behavioral norms it is natural that you will be attracted to social groups that have the same beliefs as you do. In this way you can justify your behaviors as normal and acceptable because your social group agrees with you. The pressure of these social norms comes from the collective spirit of mankind. All around the world today sex for the sake of sex has become acceptable. We all know that there is something inherently wrong with this concept but no one has been able to quite figure out what that something is; so we continue living in such a way as to allow these social norms to rule our lives. If you do not want to learn why this is wrong you should stop reading this book. Sex is the most powerful force in creation. The essence of the state of mind, intention and emotions that are all focused in that one act will create the spirit of your relationship. That moment of creation that exists when both parties are fully engaged is what they create in the spirit of themselves and their relationship. It can be very good for them or not good at all. One thing is for sure they will create the spirit of their relationship based on exactly what they are about at that moment of creation.

In the end we all have been told that celibacy is the reality we are supposed to practice; but, why?

To be intimate with someone is to create a spiritual bond with that person. When a person creates a spiritual bond with another and the intention is to feel good, not to share or create love; the bond that is created will be one that is less pure. Sex and making love is the strongest and most powerful act of creation in nature. It creates a spiritual bond that cannot be broken very easily. You need to know, what you're creating is a reflection of only what you are capable of creating. If you still have a lot of anger and other issues in your life then you will create a bond with someone and YOU WILL share that anger with them. You will also connect to their anger and it will become a very powerful connection to you too.

This is why you should work on your issues in life, cleanse your spirit and live with love; then find someone that is also capable of the same before you are intimate with him or her. This is why celibacy is so important today. It is very simple,

If you <u>need</u> to have sex, "You have work to be done".

If you have sex so you can feel better or feel less anger, "You have work to be done".

If you feel deep emotions and share them with someone you create a healthy spirit in your relationship.

There is nothing wrong with sex for the sake of sex. But you do have to be aware of the reality that it creates in your life and in the spirit of your relationship.

LUST, LOVE AND CREATION

All interactions between two people create a bond between the two people.
  These interactions can be physical actions.
  These interactions can be in thoughts.
  These interactions can be through words.

A lustful look will create through the spirit of lust. A lustful look releases cupid's arrow. Having sex without a deep love for the each other will create through the spirit of lust. Manipulating or deceiving someone with your words will create through the spirit of lust.

You should always strive to identify the moments in your day to day life when you are angry with people.

You should identify moments in your day-to-day life when you make others angry.

You should identify moments in your day-to-day life when you do not need to be angry. You need to understand why you are angry and what you are angry about? Most of the time you will realize you are angry about something insignificant.

You can prevent anger from entering your spirit!

Never allow yourself to act on some else's anger!

There are financial exchanges in life, there are personal exchanges in life and there are spiritual exchanges in life. The exchange we are all here to learn about is a spiritual exchange. A spiritual exchange is an exchange that begins with the intention behind your thoughts, words and actions. The <u>depth</u> of your intention will determine the emotional connection that goes into what you have to offer when you co-create with others.

A spiritual exchange is like pouring a cup of your spirit (feelings and thoughts) into the spirit of another person. When one person talks to another person the spirit of one person can be accepted by the other person. When one person says something that the other person accepts it is the spirit of the first person that is transferred into the spirit of the second person. This exchange is not always exactly what you expect. This is why it is so important to get to really know a person before you just trust them.

Your personal level of spiritual growth and development will determine the amount of love and light or darkness and anger you are capable of processing. The more light in your spirit and love in your heart at the moment of creation, the greater the creation that comes from your thoughts, words and actions. When you have love in your heart love will flow through your thoughts, words and actions. With only words that make you sound like a loving person you will exchange something other than love with the spirit of others.

Many people today deceive themselves into thinking and believing they have a much better spiritual reality than they actually do. It is normal to want to be better therefore believe what we want to believe. Also many people rationalize that they are better than they really are in spirit.

It is very important to know the person or people you are involved in throughout your life. Manipulative and deceptive people are very difficult to identify when you misread them initially. Their spirit can have a much bigger impact on your life than you might think. When you accept someone into your life that is not good it might take many months or even years to realize it and the damage their negative thoughts and feelings can have on you can be very destructive in nature.

THE REALITY OF LUST

Traditionally people think of lust as a reality that starts with an intimate physical action between two people. It is more than that. When two people engage in a physical relationship that has no emotional exchange or is used to control the anger that lies within you – this is lust.

Lust is when one person learns to use another in order to make his-self or her-self feel good. Lust is when a person learns to manipulate or deceive another person in order to get what he or she wants and needs in life.

Lust is that moment when being intimate that you release the anger, hatred or rage that lies within your body, spirit and soul. Less anger, hatred and rage can often be confused with love.

When a person lives day by day with a lot of anger in his or her spirit and soul a lot of anger can be released when being intimate with someone. When a person can significantly lower the darkness in their spirit they will feel a lot less anger or no anger at all – this can make you feel like, this must be love. The sudden absence of anger, hatred and rage can create an incredible bond between two people. When two people typically carry a lot of anger in their spirit this effect of creating a bond can make them feel as if they have the love needed to create a strong foundation in their relationship; but they do not.

Lust grows in a person's spirit as the result of the absence of love of self. Greed is a function of the anger that accompanies wants and needs; while lust is the hatred that accompanies a desire to use someone to make you feel better about your-self. Another level of lust is when we stare at a person with a lustful intention. This creates the spirit of lust in us and in the spirit that is in the air around us. Since we feel the feeling of lust in us we do not sense or feel the lust we are creating. Since there is no difference between what we are creating and what we feel within us, at the moment we create, it is difficult to feel that which we create. This is especially true when we live with a sprit that is not capable of holding light.

Sex is _THE_ most powerful act in creation.

The quick comparison between the lust and love is made when you think about how you feel before and after being intimate with someone.

Do you engage in sex so you can feel better afterwards?

OR

Do you express your love for someone intimately so you can share the love you feel before being intimate?

If you need to have a physical relationship your <u>need</u> is the result of a weak spirit; a spirit weak in love of self.

If you have a deep emotional moment and share this feeling by making love to someone; you are creating a mutual bond in your relationship. This bond joins your two spirits in such a way as to make the relationship stronger emotionally and spiritually.

The question you have to ask yourself is:

Are you trying to pleasure someone so they can feel better or are you both experiencing a deep <u>emotional</u> moment?

When you have a deep emotional moment (and there is nothing physical about this moment) you do not need to express yourselves physically – you will create through the love and intentions of every thought, word and action of your day to day lives.

Love is a feeling you feel that is a function of the light in your spirit.

Love is an emotion that simply exists within you and flows through you. As the light in your spirit flows into you and then you express it through the positive intentions of your thoughts, words and actions.

Love is the emotional component through which you create when your intention is to do something positive for someone else. It is about sharing love not giving it away. Love is not something that you have to take from someone. Merely engage in a moment of creation with someone when you are both feeling the same depth of emotion and you will create more of it.

All feelings and emotions have a rhythm and vibration that is unique to its-self. This is why the romantic love you feel for a life partner is different than the love you might feel for a parent or for your-self and this is still different from the love you feel for nature. Love has a vibration and rhythm that allows you to feel it. This feeling comes with the heightened sensitivity that is the result of creating a spirit that is capable of holding light. A light personal spirit has its foundation in a positive polarity. The higher your spirit's rhythm and vibration the greater your sensitivity to the spirit around you and the intentions of others.

When a person's spirit becomes capable of holding a lot of light he or she will feel more sensitive to the feelings of others. With this sensitivity comes the ability to sense and feel another person's intention when they say or do something. To sense and feel another person's spirit or to sense the intention of the spirit that is created through their words and actions is called the spiritual gift of discernment of spirit.

As people grow into this level of love and light they have a deeper commitment to caring about what others feel and how their words and actions make others feel. As they care more deeply about others they experienced a heightened ability to sense and feel the true feelings behind the words and actions of others. Quite often we learn that those that we trusted and thought had our best interest in their heart really only cared about their self and were only using us and others. This will typically make us feel angry or upset at them and our self. This will slow down your spiritual growth and development because you are feeling anger. Your spirit will not grow beyond this point until you learn to forgive the other person and your-self. When you learn to <u>accept others for who they are</u> even if they were using you or their intention was to hurt you; you will grow to the next level of light in your personal spirit.

As you continue to go through these stages of developing your spirit to accept more light into it and then learning truths that make you angry and then get past the anger your ability to discern spirit will continue to develop.

Think back through this second rule about love, sex and lust. Do you remember how many times this part of the book mentioned the importance of celibacy?

I surveyed people that read this book and very few remembered reading that word at all.

I wonder why?

There are four loves that we are creating in our lives. Each of these loves creates a purer spirit and better reality in our lives. These four loves are:

1) Love of God, Nature and Creation.
2) Love of self.
3) Love of others especially family and close friends.
4) Compassion – Love for those that wish you harm.

When a person loses his compassion for others fear and terror enters the reality of his or her life as this love becomes sealed away from his or her spirit and soul. To live in this reality is to learn to be afraid and to live with this fear in your life.

When a person continues to live in fear it is only natural that fear will grow into anger as the loss of love of others especially family and close friends becomes the next reality in your life. Anger and greed enter a person's spirit as this love becomes sealed away from his or her spirit and soul. To live in this reality is to learn how to control your anger by using things to replace the naturally good feelings that no longer exist in your life. To have wants and needs for things is to experience the spirit of greed.

As the process of a broken spirit continues it is only natural to love your love of self. Hatred is the feeling that replaces love self. This is when people use other people to replace the natural feeling that a person used to live with before their spirit and soul were sealed into this darker reality.

The final love lost is love of God, Nature and Creation. This is the love that many today are striving to grow into. The healing of this part of our collective spirit can be seen in mankind's unprecedented attempts to protect animals and nature as well as our desire to learn more about God. When a person loses this love he or she replaces the natural feeling of love of God, Nature and Creation with cravings as they become overwhelmed with the need to have things or to use people to make them feel good again.

Mankind has been working for 2,000 years to get to this point where we are now working together to make this world a better place. Groups of people from all around the world are now working together to save whales and dolphins, protect animals from abusive owners, find alternative sources of fuel to power the world and make people's lives better. This reality in the world is an example of how we are growing into this first love that we will have to manifest in our lives and then let it become a reality in our lives.

The next reality that future generations are going to have to deal with is the healing of our love of self.

Rule #3 – DON'T MAKE DEALS WITH GOD

QUESTIONS AND TIPS TO THINK ABOUT AS YOU READ RULE #3

God created creation so we could learn the power of creation that flows through our thoughts, words and actions. Always asking God to help us and to rely on God, nature the universe or creation to just make things happen is not what life is all about. Life is about us, you and me creating our own reality; thereby making the world a better place.

While it may be a rule to not just ask God to make your life better – it is natural to do so. But do not expect that God will just make it better for you and you do not have to do your part.

Did you ever ask God to find you a new car, apartment of other physical thing you felt you needed?

Did you ever make a deal with God to get you out of a bad situation and then promise to go to church on Sunday or to change your way life in some way?

Did you ever ask God to just fix a relationship for you?

After asking for God's help did you receive thoughts that guided you to do something to make it happen?

Did you follow the guidance you were given?

If yes, how did you follow this guidance?

Were you ever so focused on accomplishing something so important that, nothing else mattered?

Were you so focused on achieving that something that it consumed your every thought, word and action?

Is it possible that when you are consumed by creating what you need in life; that perhaps this is what we are here to learn to do?

Are we supposed to be consumed and then to learn to overcome being consumed by wanting, needing, desiring or craving things so we can learn to hunger to do the right thing in life?

Are we supposed to just do what we know is the right thing to do in the first place?

RULE #3 - MAKING PROMISES TO GOD vs. JUST DOING WHAT WE KNOW IS THE RIGHT THING TO DO

Sometimes the challenges in life become so difficult that we need help. We reach deep in our hearts and just ask for help. This help will be there but you have to know how to allow yourself to be guided to what you need in order to find your way out of the situation you created.

Do you rely on God or some other deity to help you throughout your day?

Do you make promises to the universe, nature or God so they can use their control to make your life better?

Many people believe they should make a deal with God by promising they will go to church on Sunday, make a charitable donation or make some other temporary change in their life as long as God gives them something they crave, desire, want or need. While there are times when this works there is a greater lesson to be learned from life, than to just expect God to make your life better.

<u>MAKING A DEAL WITH GOD IS NOT HOW CREATION WORKS.</u>

All you have to do to make an improvement in your life is just simply make the change and then it will happen. You can change your life. The changes you need to make will happen when you are serious about making them. When you sincerely want to make a change and are willing to do whatever it takes to change and then do whatever it takes – the changes will happen. There is a moment in everyone's life when we realize that it is time. It is at this moment in time that we are ready to begin the quest to find our light. At this moment we realize that we have been rationalizing that the hurtful things we do to others were wrong. With this realization we have the strength to change our spirit.

You do not have to make a deal with God like you would your boss or someone you are trying to buy or sell something with.

We are here to make changes in our lives; but we have to make them. It is not always about God or the universe or nature doing it for us. God is here to help but we are here to make our own reality in our life.

We change our reality by dealing with our issues in life and allowing our spirit to grow into a light-based reality. We co-create our lives through every exchange we make when we interact with others. When we interact with nature as well as people we create from the purpose we live with in every thought, word or action.

You do not have to make a deal with God.

You just have to do what you know you should do in life and everything will fall into place. You should work hard, live within your means and know what the right thing to do is and then just simply do what you know it right. We all know the right things to do in life but sometimes it is just difficult to get over the hurdles that life places in front of us. When we ask God for help with these hurdles he will offer us guidance but we have to do the work. When people continually strive to get past some of life's hurdles but just don't seem to be able to make it happen on their own God, nature and creation will always be there to help. When your commitment and effort is sincere you do not have to ask for the help you deserve, it will just be there. Of course this is much easier said than done – perhaps that is why we are here – perhaps this is what we are here to learn to do!!!

It is difficult to just simply do the right thing in your day to day life when your spirit is not strong enough to just do what you know is right. Re-creating your spirit is the first step. You do have to learn to re-create your spirit so you can make your life better. Then you can make the world a better place for everyone to live in.

This is not to say that you should not pray to God and ask for guidance. Just don't believe that you should try to make a deal with God in order to make a change in your life. It is not like giving money to get exactly what you want in life. It is about committing your spirit and soul to what you want and then accepting what you receive or the change in your life. To commit your spirit and soul completely to something or someone is to love with all your heart, body, mind and strength. Only a spirit that is strong enough to hold is capable of loving completely and then committing yourself to doing the right thing. To hunger for righteousness is to commit your spirit and soul to doing the right thing. When you are overcome with a hunger to do the right thing you are on the right path to healing your spirit.

Example:

Some people convince themselves that they are doing everything right because they talk about their intentions and try to convince themselves and others that their intentions are always righteous. Some even believe they can have multiple intentions when they are creating as if they can do the wrong thing for the right reasons and still create a righteous spirit. It does not work this way. The lowest vibrating part of your intention is what will create in your spirit. You cannot say that you are doing something for everyone else's benefit or a highest good and then charge people a lot of money for the service you are providing and then expect to create a spirit that is based on your good intention. If the reality that is deep inside you is to make money then you will make money but not create a spirit that is filled with light. You cannot fool creation (God) like this. This is why some people say that God knows what is in your heart.

When you feel like your back is up against the wall and all you want in life is to have what you need, your intention and what it needs in order to manifest will be there for you. When a person asks God to give him a bigger boat or a bigger house, when the one they currently have is enough (even if they feel like they need more) you might get it but you also might regret it. When you act on wants and needs in your life you can work hard to get them; but you will have to work extra hard for it and you will continue paying for it for a very long time. It is like when you buy a bigger house you will have to pay more for utilities, more for insurance, spend more time cleaning and maintaining the house. Instead if you downsized when buying the house you would have more money left at the end of the week and more time to relax and enjoy life's moments. Not everyone can just relax and enjoy life's moments; when some people just try to relax their wants, needs and desires kick in and they have to go and satisfy their needs to have more than, what should be enough. Instead of feeding their peace of mind they feed their wants and needs. When you act on wants, needs, desires and cravings you will sacrifice the loves you need to feel good without these things.

These manifestations (MAN-ifestations) are things that you think and feel you need because your spirit is not capable of holding light therefore you want, need, desire and crave things to make you feel good instead of being able to just let yourself feel good. The positive loving spirit of God (creation) does not work at this level. The spirit of nature provides what you need to survive while in a darker state and to provide you with the guidance you need to change when you are ready to grow out of a need based reality and lifestyle.

To mend a broken spirit and a broken heart is to experience the healing process - Forgive and Live with Love. If you pray to God or ask for help healing your spirit and soul you will receive the guidance you need to heal from God as it comes through the spirit of nature. If you ask for things to make you feel better about yourself you may get what you want but you are not getting those things directly from God; but from God's creation; the spirit of nature.

A prayer should be a request for God to help you on your path to complete your quest to create a bright light in your spirit. This is the theme of the catholic prayer called the "Our Father". It is all about asking God to help us by forgiving us for hurting others and explains that we will be forgiven to the same level of forgiveness as we have forgiven those that hurt us. It is about the reality that we will create an amount of forgiveness for ourselves that is equal to the amount of forgiveness that we create when we forgive others. This is the exchange we make as we learn to forgive. The exchange is about the depth of sincerity that we commit from our heart when we ask for forgiveness. Then we will create forgiveness in our spirit that is a reflection of the heartfelt commitment that we made when asking for forgiveness.

THIS IS HOW CREATION WORKS – If we want to be forgiven we have to forgive those that hurt us. This is how we change our spirits rhythm, vibration and polarity.

You lose your spirit's capability to hold light when:

You reach deep into your heart with anger or resentment, hatred or rage and say or think, "I will never forgive someone".

Your spirit is not capable of holding light when:

Your intention in an exchange is to take the most or to make the most by giving or doing the least; with no emotion or compassion you are not creating a healthy spirit for your-self, for all of mankind or contributing to the overall health of the ambient spirit that exists in the world. This is how greed works through the interactions of a person's day to day life.

You begin the process of transforming your spirit from dark to light by cleansing the darkness from it. You begin this quest to create light when:

You forgive someone with the same strength and commitment as you did when you created the seal that sealed your spirit into a darker reality.

Your spirit is capable of holding light when:

When you are truly grateful for the opportunity to share something with someone and generous in giving of yourself during this exchange you are creating a better you, a healthier personal spirit (one that is capable of creating love and light) and manifest positive ambient spirit.

When on your journey into a darker reality the moments in your life define your existence; when you start you quest you begin to learn how to allow your spirit's existence to define the moments in your life.

Being generous and grateful is the polar opposite of greed.

When you ask for God to help you to create forgiveness in your spirit you are asking for guidance and it will be there for you. You do not have to make a deal with God you merely have to let the process of creation work thought you. Then you have to follow his lead. It can be a challenge to learn to follow these more positive thoughts but over time, you will learn. These changes do not happen overnight; but over time we will find the peace we all want and need in our lives.

RULE #4 – REVENGE - DON'T VOLLEY SOMEONE ELSE'S ANGER

QUESTIONS AND TIPS TO THINK ABOUT AS YOU READ RULE #4

Did you ever get into a discussion that grew into a debate that grew into an argument and then into a fight?

Did you ever feel the change in the spirit of the room as this happens?

Did you ever walk into a room and just feel the positive nature of the people in the room as if you just wanted to get to know everyone and become their friend?

Did you ever feel the spirit of a room change shortly after someone turned on some music or a band began to play?

These questions are all about your ability to sense and feel the spirit of a room (some people refer to this as discerning spirit). This is the first level of sensitivity we all feel. It is important to know how this ability to sense and feel works. As your personal spirit interacts with the spirit of others the spirit of the other person becomes a part of your spirit; then you feel what exists in the other person. The same is true of the spirit that exists in a room you enter. When you enter a room where others have been talking the spirit of their words fill the air in the room and you will feel the nature of their discussion.

These sensing skills are one of the first you will learn because they are the most important skills you will need on your quest to heal your spirit and soul.

RULE #4 – REVENGE - DON'T VOLLEY SOMEONE ELSE'S ANGER

HOW TO RESPOND TO SOMEONE ELSE'S ANGER OR DESTRUCTIVE SPIRIT.

DO NOT – NEVER EVER – VOLLEY SOMEONE ELSE'S ANGER BACK TO THEM.

DO NOT ALLOW SOMEONE ELSE TO FORCE THE ANGER OF THEIR SPIRIT INTO YOUR SPIRIT.

DO NOT EVER ACT ON SOMEONE ELSE'S ANGER TOWARDS YOU.

REVENGE WILL ONLY PERPETUATE THE EXISTENCE OF THE RAGE THAT WAS CREATED IN THE FIRST PLACE. STOP PASSING THIS SPIRIT FORWARD.

HOW ANGER GROWS WHEN WE VOLLEY IT

When someone whose spirit is filled with anger, hatred or rage approaches you with an intention to share the darkness of their spirit with you – you must be very very careful to not let this person transfer his or her anger from their spirit into yours.

This person will only be able to hurt your spirit if he or she can get you to accept the darkness that lives within them and then get you to act on their anger, hatred or rage.

The key is to not allow the spirit of anger to enter into your spirit. If it does, do not act on it either verbally or physically. Acting on someone else's anger is how the spiritual bond is created.

If they are not able to force their spirit into you by using fear and bullying tactics to force their will on you, they will try to verbally abuse you as they strive to share their anger with you. If they are unsuccessful in transferring their anger and hatred through verbal abuse they may become physical. The best way to prevent them from making you act on the anger, hatred and rage they live with, all day long every day of their life, is to simply turn the other cheek. Do not act in a hostile or unforgiving way just simply walk away and leave them to their misery and suffering.

If you react to their actions with the same spirit of anger then you will have co-created a bond with this person and will then share their pain and suffering until you learn to cleanse your spirit and soul. One way to cleanse your spirit is to use the process of forgiveness.

Revenge is the motivator that encourages a person to act when in an envious state of mind. Vengeance is the essence of the spirit of envy while turning the other cheek is the de-motivator that prevents the creation of a spiritual bond with someone that is in this state of mind (reality of creation).

Today there is a common phrase that is supposed to relate to how people volley hatred and rage back and forth at one another. That phrase is, "A Holy War". There is nothing holy about war. But the spirit of war and its conflict is about how two countries or ideologies volley the hate that is at the foundation of the spirit of way back and forth. Too many people it is about how they strive to force their belief or ideology onto others. The spirit of this action can be very detrimental to the overall collective spirit of mankind. It is one thing to have an opinion about what you want or believe in. It is a whole new reality to try to force someone else to believe what you believe. To express your opinion and to be open to what others have to say is a much greater and will free your spirit. To close your mind to what others have to say or to what others believe will imprison your spirit. To take it to the next level and to try to force your opinion on others will lock the door on the cell in which you have imprisoned your spirit. It is the action and the depth of it that will determine the length of the jail term you are giving your-self. I hope you can see how fear, anger, hatred and rage can imprison you and then rule your life like a warden rules a prison or kings of the past ruled their lands.

A COUPLE OF EXAMPLES OF HOW PEOPLE FORCE THEIR WILL ON OTHERS AND THEN VOLLEY THE SPIRIT OF ANGER

Example #1 – The direct assault

When a person approaches you and introduces him-self or her-self and then starts a conversation. The conversation might focus on something you did or are doing. If, what you are doing is creating a problem for this other person. He will mention that it is upsetting him as his voice raises and his anger enters the spirit of the conversation. When you feel this anger you must recognize that it is not coming from your personal spirit and not act on it by raising your voice or contributing to the conversation. Try to redirect the conversation to something positive or if the angry person is directing the conversation towards something you did specifically try to apologize to eliminate the anger in the conversation. If this person harbors a lot of rage and continues increasing the anger in the spirit of the conversation it is very important that you not let this rage consume your spirit. If you put a spin on the conversation you can start talking about how great it is to see this person and how nice it is to have a chance to talk with him or her. What this does is it prevents the anger this person is trying to share with you from entering your spirit. It also forces the angry person to keep his or her anger within his or her spirit. It is like bottling them up in their own rage.

When two people have a conversation that escalates from a discussion to a debate and then to an argument they are accepting anger from one another and then volleying it back and forth as if to feed off the other persons feelings. This escalation of the spirit of the conversation is the cause of the bad feelings between the two people. By simply recognizing the anger in the spirit of the conversation and then changing the spirit of your words and actions you can prevent the argument and maintain a healthy conversation with your friends.

Example #2

Feeding someone anger while masking it with love

Three people can engage in a conversation and act like they all agree with one another. But one person might not. Even though this person's words may sound like she is agreeing with the other two her intention and thoughts are not in agreement with the other two. Therefore the spirit of her words is anger-based, manipulative and deceptive. While carrying on the discussion this person that does not agree can say words that sound like they agree but actually create the spirit of disagreement. When the other two people feel this spirit of disagreement one will start to argue with the other and actually be making the point the other person would have made but does not want to come out from behind the words that masked her true intentions. This is what I call hiding behind a mask of deception. When the other two people begin arguing the third person will just sit quietly waiting for the opportunity to interrupt and act like a mediator or facilitator; the other two will not even realize they were manipulated by the deceptive spirit of the third person's words.

RULE #5 –LOVE COMPLETELY ESPECIALLY THOSE THAT WISH YOU HARM

QUESTIONS AND TIPS TO THINK ABOUT AS YOU READ RULE #5

When you meet someone and you greet them with a hello or a friendly hug –

Do you say hello how are you with a serious commitment to wanting to know how they are doing?

When you greet someone do you share a friendly hug and truly hug them with an intention to share your-self with them in that moment? Do you really mean it or is it just a formality?

How do you create the spirit of love in your conversations with others?

Have you ever just felt love in a conversation without the need to try to create it?

RULE #5 –LOVE COMPLETELY ESPECIALLY THOSE THAT WISH YOU HARM

When a person tries to hurt you by sharing the darkness of their spirit with you the best way to protect your spirit is to love them completely. In this case the best defense is a strong offense.

By sharing love with a person that is trying to share anger with you; you will prevent a spiritual bond from forming. Love and anger are nature's opposites. They have opposite polarities. Therefore a spiritual bond cannot be created when these two forces of creation meet.

In order for a spiritual bond to occur two people must express themselves through similar spirits.

Love and light will bond with love and light.

The darkness of anger will bond with the darkness of anger.

Light and dark will repel one another and no spiritual bond will be co-created.

Love truly is the answer to so many of this world's problems. But to love deeply means to develop a spirit that is capable of loving deeply.

To love someone that loves you is easy and will create some light in your spirit. But to love someone that wants to hurt you, to love someone whose lifestyle is very different from your own and might be hurtful towards you or others is the challenge that will create a bright light in your personal spirit. To love someone that is not easy to love will always give you a spiritual reward that is much greater than to love someone that is easy to love.

Just like forgiving someone and truly meaning it. To forgive for the sole purpose of forgiving and with no ulterior motive will create forgiveness in your personal spirit. This is how God forgives you when you have forgiven others. To truly love someone no matter what their beliefs or what they do to you or to others is to love in such a way as to create a very powerful love in you.

Just like forgiveness requires an intention to forgive that is pure your love for someone has to be equally pure. You cannot love someone because it is the right thing to do – you have to love because you love. There is a big difference between loving because you are supposed to and forgiving and loving because you truly forgive someone and then love them because you can.

BEGIN CREATING THE LOVE BASED SPIRIT THAT WILL BE THE FOUNDATION OF THE SPIRIT THAT WILL PROPEL US INTO THE FUTURE

RULE #6 – DO NOT BE AFRAID TO CRY OR MOURN A LOSS. TRYING TO PUT ON A HAPPY FACE SO OTHERS WILL THINK YOU ARE STRONG WHEN FACED WITH SORROW WILL ONLY PREVENT YOU FROM CREATING YOUR PERSONAL SPIRIT TO BE AS HEALTHY AS IT CAN BE.

Do you remember a time in your life when you were afraid? When you were so afraid that you felt terrified. Below write a few words that you might remember from this moment.

Do you remember how you reacted to this moment?

Did you cry?

Were you so overwhelmed with emotions that you felt like you might never stop crying? Did you stop crying? Did you decide to never cry again?

If yes, that's Ok. Many do.

Now that you know that your feelings will create your personal spirit – What do you think this moment in your life created in you?

RULE #6 – LET GO OF THE SADNESS, THE SORROW AND THE FEAR

THE IMPORTANCE OF RELEASING THE SORROS AND THE FEAR SO YOU CAN CREATE A SPIRIT THAT IS READY TO HOLD LIGHT

When people live in an environment that is consumed by anger, hatred and rage it is only natural that people in that environment will also be filled with and act on anger, hatred and rage. When this happens they will hurt those around them. This is just how an anger-based spirit works. It infects the spirit of those that are weaker in spirit like a plague infects the human body.

When others act on the anger, hatred and rage within them they will try to take the light from the spirit of others. When a person with a light based spirit is no longer strong enough to withstand the actions of others they will naturally lose their light. If a person with anger can share the fear that lives within them with someone else the good person will feel their fear. When fear grows in this good person a fight or flight mechanism within them will be triggered. When flight is no longer an option he or she will have to fight and usually this leads to creating a personal spirit that is no longer without fear. If the environment this person lives in does not change fear will usually become a permanent reality in this good person spirit as he or she loses the light that used to motivate and guide their actions. When he or she cannot escape the anger-based environment that exists it is only natural that the light in their spirit will be replaced with a spirit that is no longer capable of holding light.

People then learn to accept fear and the lower vibrating realities that come with it. To live with fear is to live with a sense of being afraid. Over time people accept this feeling as if it is normal. It is normal because it is a part of the collective spirit that they are now a part of. When living with this sense of being afraid you learn to feel the fear and do what you have to do in life anyways. When people are on their quest to find their light they have to learn to replace the fear with the comfort they felt in life that existed when fear did not exist. In order to transform a spirit that is not capable of holding light into one that is no longer afraid you have to learn to cry. Crying can be very powerful and very healing. Crying is a way of letting go of the past and allowing the feelings that you had to deny in order to live in the anger and fear-based environment, to leave your spirit. In order to live with fear you have to live with a certain amount of denial that it exists within you.

When you lose your ability to mourn a loss you are simply doing what you have to do in order to survive in an environment that cannot support a light-based spirit. As you grow older it is only normal to leave that hurtful environment but you still live with the effects of it. There will come a point in time when you will be able to grow into a healthy and more mature spirit. When that time comes you will learn to deal with the issues that came out of your past as you learn to forgive and love again. Part of this process of healing is to remember and even relive these past experiences. As you relive and grow beyond these past experiences you will have to learn to let yourself mourn the losses you felt and to live with love again. As you cleanse your spirit by crying it is like making room for happiness to replace the sadness that used to reside in your spirit. This will then allow your spirit to regain the strength it needs to hold light again.

The most important thing you have to while feeling all the emotions that are now free for you to feel again is to use them to forgive those that hurt you in the first place. Forgiveness will reverse the polarity of your spirit thereby allowing you create a love-based spirit.

RULE #7 – FORGIVE, FORGIVE, FORGIVE – FORGIVE OTHERS, FORGIVE YOUR-SELF AND THEN FORGIVE AGAIN

QUESTIONS AND TIPS TO THINK ABOUT AS YOU READ RULE #7

Did you ever forgive someone that just annoyed you?

Did you ever forgive someone that hurt you to the core of your being?

Which was easier?

When you forgive someone do you just say the words and not really mean it?

When you forgive someone do you reach deep into your-self and commit a lot of love into it?

Committing a lot of love or a little love to your creations - which do you think created the greatest amount of forgiveness in your spirit and soul?

RULE #7 – FORGIVE, FORGIVE, FORGIVE – FORGIVE OTHERS, FORGIVE YOUR-SELF AND THEN FORGIVE AGAIN

THE IMPORTANCE OF FORGIVENESS

Love and forgiveness are very closely linked to one another in our spirit and in the process of forgiveness. When a person loses the ability to love, he or she will lose the ability to create through love. Without the ability to create through love the ability to forgive will be limited and eventually lost. Without love and forgiveness in your spirit; your spirit cannot hold light. Without the ability to hold light your spirit will exist in the darkness of anger. The prophecy, "The Revelation of Christ" refers to seven seals that seal a book. This book with seven seals represents your soul consciousness when it is sealed away from the light side of the heavens.

Forgiveness is so vital to a healthy spirit that you cannot live with love or create light without it.

To create forgiveness in your spirit you must use love to create the spirit of forgiveness in your thoughts, words and actions. The more love you put into the forgiveness you seek, the more forgiveness you will create. You can look someone in the eye and discuss the situation that made you unable to forgive them or just do it with your thoughts. In many cases it is not feasible to meet someone face to face so the process can be completed simply with your thoughts and feelings about the person and situation you experienced with him or her.

All the aspects of you, of your personality, that you create must have a foundation in love. It is the depth of love that you put into your life that will determine what your life will be all about. Love will define the reality of your life.

If you want to feel more accepted by others you will need to accept others into your life and then you will create acceptance in your spirit. It is the love that you put into accepting others that will be the love that you will feel from others after you have created it. When you have completely accepted others for who they are you feel accepted by others and others will feel accepted by you. This is the foundation that you need to create in your spirit in order to create healthier relationships.

If you want to create peace of mind for yourself you must create peace through the love in your heart. The peace you will feel will be a function of the love that you combine with the intention (that flows from within you) to be at peace in your life. As you create it through your thoughts, words and actions you will feel more at peace with those around you.

The process of forgiveness starts where you want it to start. You can seek forgiveness from others or forgive others for what they have done to you. It really does not matter as long as you just do it.

Forgiveness may start out small with a weak intention and no real commitment to it and that is OK. As long as you start, it will grow inside of you and over time you will become more sincere in your attempts to forgive or be forgiven.

Over time you will realize that you have to forgive yourself for things that you feel guilty about. Forgiving your self is one of the more difficult ones for many people. It is a necessary part of the process.

As you continue forgiving yourself and others or seeking forgiveness for what you have done to others you will receive forgiveness in your spirit. As a result of creating forgiveness in your spirit, your spirit will become stronger and more capable of holding light. As your spirit holds enough light in it you will naturally feel the love, which is this light. As you continue to use this love and light to continue the process forgiveness you will create an even stronger spirit that is capable of holding even more light.

As this process of re-creating your spirit continues you will create a foundation of forgiveness and love in your spirit. As this foundation continues to grow you will use it to create more aspects of you and your personality through it.

As you live with love in your heart and light in your spirit you will naturally become more sensitive to the thoughts, words and actions of others. This is great when others have peaceful and love-based thoughts, words and actions; but when someone creates a spirit with an intention that is hurtful towards you, your heightened sensitivity may work against you. The hurt you will feel will require you to continue forgiving those that wish you harm and hurt you. This hurt may come as a bit of a surprise because many people think and believe, when they have completed this process of forgive and live with love and that they are done. The need to maintain love, light and forgiveness in your spirit must be committed too with vigilance.

If you do not use it you will lose it.

The next level of creation is co-creation. When you have effectively created a forgiving spirit within you those that were involved with your act of forgiveness will now feel differently towards you. They may not have looked you in the eye as you asked for forgiveness but they will feel a difference in the relationship or interaction you had with them. Over time they may recognize that they feel guilty for their role in the experience that hurt you or may not feel as hurt by your actions if you did something hurtful to him or her. This person will then seek forgiveness from you. When they complete the process of forgiveness the two spirits that existed in a polarizing reality will now be attracted to one another again. This the next level reality is what we have to strive to create.

Ultimately we need to create stronger relationships between large groups and organizations that have been carrying anger, hatred, rage or even envy towards one another. The ultimate reality that has to be created is for Israel and Islam, the United States and Russia, All the American Indians and the rest of the United States to forgive one another collectively. When the spirit of forgiveness exists between these nations and all the people of the world, the world will be ready to find peace of mind and peace on earth.

We can create a forgiving collective spirit of mankind and then manifest true love in the world. Then and only then will we have a loving God to feed us the love that we need.

RULE #8 – LOVE DEEPLY IN EVERYTHING YOU SAY, THINK AND DO

QUESTIONS AND TIPS TO THINK ABOUT AS YOU READ RULE #8

Love and Creation is not about romantic love. It is about experiencing the love that flows from the source of all emotions through you and so you can manifest it into the ambient spirit of the world (into the air all around us). It is a love that you can share at any moment in the day when you say something very positive to someone and truly, even deeply, mean what you say. The depth of your commitment to what you say will manifest the spirit of your words into the world. This is how to make (manifest) love in the spirit of the world.

When was the last time you told someone you love them?

Did you really mean it or did you just say it because it was the right thing to say at the moment?

How often do you say something that you feel deeply about?

How often to you speak with so much sincerity that you can feel the sincerity flowing through your words?

When was the last time you realized that everyone was listening to what you were saying, as if hanging on every word?

When was the last time you knew that you filled the room with your spirit as you talked about something you were passionate about?

Could you feel the love flow out from your body to the person or people that you were expressing your love for?

When was the last time you shared a moment of deep felt love with someone?

Have you ever just given someone a hug and truly shared a moment where you felt the love of the moment?

RULE #8 – LOVE DEEPLY IN EVERYTHING YOU SAY, THINK AND DO

As a person lives in a hurtful environment (at home, in a community or other place where you feel you cannot escape from) it is only natural to lose your ability to love those around you and then lose your ability to forgive them for the hurtful things they do to you and to others around you. When your spirit is sealed into this darker reality it is natural to rationalize that the suffering you feel comes from the love and other positive emotions you live with. This rationalizing begins with the rationale that the hurt you feel comes from the love and other positive feelings and emotions that exist(ed) in your life.

When the hurt becomes more than you can bare you will simply give your positive feelings and emotions away as you learn to live with lesser emotions. This leads to not being able to forgive others for creating the hurtful environment. This is how you begin to create a seal that will prevent your spirit from holding light. When you lose your light and then lose your capability to forgive you create your spiritual seal. Now you live with a personal spirit that is dark and the reality that accompanies it throughout your life.

After a person learns the process of forgiveness and cleanses his or her spirit of the darkness they lived in and re-create's his or her spirit in such a way as to make it stronger and more capable of holding light – the next step is to learn to live with love again.

It is natural to remember only the hurt that came with having these positive feelings in the past. Therefore it is only natural to resist allowing yourself to feel them again. Rest assured it will happen; you will feel this natural love again.

As a person begins the quest into light it is natural too, one day, just feel really great, it is like a feeling that was lost and now you found it again. You will feel like celebrating in the same way you used to celebrate when you found a lost coin. But this feeling will just come from out of nowhere. For no reason at all you will just feel good. This is when you know that your spirit has been filled with light.

It is natural to want to hold onto that feeling and not want to let it go. Eventually you will realize that you are supposed to let go of it and share it with others. You will not want to give it away as you might have done in past relationships. This love, you will want to keep and share with others. When you learn to share love with every thought, word and action you will have completed the cycle of creating light in your spirit and love in your heart. It is evolutionary to allow yourself to feel good again. This is how we evolve through creation. As we learn to create a better spirit we will just evolve into a better reality in our lives.

You just have to let the love flow and it will change your life. But first you have to create your personal spirit in such a way as to be able to hold the light that will feed you love.

Now you are capable of following this seventh rule of creation - love deeply in everything you say, think and do.

The more you share your love with others and live with love as a purpose in life the stronger your spirit will become as your light begins to shine brightly.

RULE #9 - BE RIGHTEOUS

QUESTIONS AND TIPS TO THINK ABOUT AS YOU READ RULE #9

Do you know the difference between right and wrong? Of course you do!

How many times throughout the day do you know that you are doing something that you just know is not the right thing to do but do it anyways?

How many times throughout the day do you know what the right thing to do is and then do it?

How many times a day do you know the right thing to do and then find an excuse to not do it or just do not even try? This is rationalizing!

Do you believe that if it feels right that you should just do it?

Why does it just feel right to do something that you just know is the wrong thing to do?

Can your thoughts and feelings deceive you into thinking that it is right to do the wrong thing? Again this is rationalizing!

RULE #9 - BE RIGHTEOUS – ALWAYS STRIVE TO JUST DO THE RIGHT THING. YOU WILL NATURALLY LIVE WITH AN INTENTION TO ALWAYS DO WHAT YOU KNOW TO BE THE RIGHT THING TO DO

Many people use the phrase righteous but few actually define it. It is simply doing what you know is the right thing to do in your life. It is that something that does not always feel like the right thing to do but in your heart you know what is right. As people begin to grow a lighter spirit it is natural to expand your understanding of right and wrong and develop the willpower that will make it easier to do the right thing in your life. As a matter of fact when your spirit is filled with light you will be motivated to just do the right thing. It will feel very wrong to not help others and do what is best for yourself and for others.

You see the hurtful things people do throughout their day to day interactions with others is just the best they can do. When their spirit is broken and not able to hold light people do not sense and feel the pain they are causing. Therefore it does not feel wrong to do something that hurts someone else. A person that begins to hold light will feel sympathy towards others but still try to do what is best for him-self or her-self. A person whose spirit is filled with a light that shines brightly will live to do what is best for others and will no longer worry about his or her own personal wants, needs or desires. As your light becomes bright your sympathy will grow into empathy as you become capable of sensing the pain that others live with. When you can feel someone else's sadness you will not want to make them sad because it will make you sad.

This feeling of what is right and wrong is a feeling that comes from the collective spirit. The thoughts that rationalize our actions comes from the collective consciousness. We are all a part of a collective spirit. The spirit in which we are naturally connected to, is the spirit of others whose spirits are of the same rhythm and vibration as ours (the same intensity of light or dark). If a person has a dark spirit it is only natural that this person's spirit will be a part of others that are the same. A person with a light spirit will naturally be connected to those that have light in their spirit also. People with a light spirit have the capability to be connected to a larger part of the collective spirit of mankind and a higher consciousness than those that live with a spirit that is not capable of holding light. A person with a light spirit is connected to those that have a spirit equal too and darker than their own. This is true of all levels of light and dark. You are connected to the collective of those whose spirit is the same or similar to your own and those who have a spirit with a lower rhythm and vibration.

This is why it is natural for a person whose spirit is capable of holding light to have a choice to be angry or can chose to reject the thoughts and feelings that allow anger to enter their spirit and life. But a person whose spirit is not capable of holding light cannot choose to love. A person whose spirit is not capable of holding light is capable of experiencing a certain level of anger or more anger but not love; and the consciousness that accompanies it.

The connection a person has to others whom they bond with and the natural connection that comes with this level of light their spirit is capable of holding:

- Will determine how you live your life.
- Will determine the thoughts and feelings they experience throughout their day-to-day interactions with others.
- Will motivate your thoughts, words and actions. It is that which creates the reality that is your life.

These connections are spiritual connections (or bonds) therefore they impact your day-to-day and moment-to-moment feelings, thoughts, words and actions. These connections to your collective will either help or hinder your chances to say, think and do the right things in your life.

Being righteous is not always about not doing what feels right but it is about not doing what we know is or can be hurtful to others. The more you do the right thing the better you will feel. IT is like you will feel good all day long. Some people do hurtful things so they can immediately receive a feeling that makes them feel better than they did before they did something hurtful. The release of a bad feeling that occurs when you do something hurtful to others is not the right way to live. But for some people the hurt they feel is so intense the only way they can release their pain is by hurting others. When you do the fight things throughout your life you create a spirit that is healthier and therefore you make your-self feel better all the time. Each good thing you do adds a little goodness to your spirit. Over time the bad goes away as it is replaced with love and compassion.

This is why the law of creation states that you must always strive to love completely and then to share that love with others. This is why you must always allow the best possible intention to flow through you in everything you say, think and do.

A person who grows a spirit that allows love and light to naturally flow through him or her will feel deeply about doing the right thing. As a person hungers of righteousness the depth of emotion needed to create righteousness in his or her spirit will exist. You have to hunger for righteousness to overcome the cravings of gluttony. After you have created forgiveness, love and righteousness in your personal spirit it is only natural to be grateful for the opportunity to be generous with your things as well as with your emotions and your spirit.

Please always think before you speak and act. Think about what you are about to do and if there is a better way to say it or to do it.

RULE #10 – GIVE GENEROUSLY AND BE GRATEFUL

QUESTIONS AND TIPS TO THINK ABOUT AS YOU READ RULE #10

When you buy something do you feel as if you should always pay no more than the price marked for it?

When you buy something do you feel as if you should make sure you are getting your money's worth?

Think about the above two questions and then describe your feelings as it relates to something as simple as buying an item at the store?

Do you remember the first time you left some extra money on the counter at a grocery store or restaurant for someone who might need it?

The first time you did it was it easy to just leave money for someone else?

Do you think about leaving money for others very often?

What happens when these thoughts enter your mind?

Did it take a while for these generous thoughts to sink in and then, one day, you just did it?

Where do you think these thoughts and feelings that motivate you to act in a generous way, or to not act in a generous way, come from?

RULE #10 – GIVE GENEROUSLY AND BE GRATEFUL AS OFTEN AS YOU POSSIBLY CAN

If you think about it – the entire system of life that has been created to honor our physical life and to disregard our spiritual and emotional life has existed for thousands of years. It is a state of mind that affected everyone in the world. The need to have coins in our pockets has grown to so outweigh respect for others and creating relationships that it created an imbalance in our lives, both individually and collectively. The system was designed to take from the earth that which is the rarest and to use it to determine if an individual person's value was better than another's. The whole concept of how much gold or silver a person has in their pocket instead of how much good they do for others is what determines value and what is important to society. So naturally mankind chooses a mineral from the earth that is believed to be the rarest and then uses it to compare one person's worth to another as if their life has no meaning unless they have this rare mineral. Our complete survival depends on having this rare mineral or the paper that represents it in our life. In the end we feel more compelled to have this paper in our pocket than to help our fellow man in a time of need. Our first thoughts are always, "How much will it cost" and, "Will I have enough money to do what I want or need, to have what I desire or crave". It is as if we should be afraid to live without it. Perhaps the fear we live with is the fear of having to deal the issues in our lives that we cover up by buying things.

We really do not even feel grateful for what we have any more. We assume that we should get what we want and need as if it should be provided for us. We are supposed to work for what we get in life but we need to enjoy what we are doing. We need to create happiness in our jobs and careers. We need to create a life filled with something more than just having what we want and need and expecting it to be there as if this is enough to make my life whole.

One of the first steps to creating a better life for your-self is to learn to be grateful for what you have and to give generously. To overcome those thoughts that tells us to not share and to not pay it forward. When you take what you want and need with no regard for others and with no sense of being grateful for what you have, you create a different feeling in your spirit. This is a feeling of deserving what you have. An exchange like this creates a lower vibrating personal spirit and through the interaction creates a loser vibration within the collective spirit and manifests greed in the aid around us.

We feel we deserve what we have whether on welfare and food stamps or being the CEO of a successful company. It is the feeling that we feel we, "deserve" that will be the biggest barrier to overcome in order to create gratefulness and generosity in your spirit. It all starts with one simple act of kindness. A true act of kindness is one that you do and then no one knows you did it. When you do something kind and you are anonymous, you will create a positive vibration in your spirit as the result of the act of kindness. If you do something nice for someone and then tell everyone or in some other way let everyone know you did it; you will receive this earthly reward from others. Trust me, a pat on the back may make you feel good for a little while but over time that feeling will go away. When a pat on the back no longer feels as good as it did the first time you will need to do something more self-centered in order to get what you need to make you feel good. This process of wanting and needing is what you must to overcome in order to let generosity become a reality in your life.

A true act of kindness will create something in your spirit that you can feed off of for as long as you continue to do more of the same. This spiritual nourishment will make you just feel good for no reason at all.

When you are sitting in an open space and over hear a conversation about a person that needs some money to pay her rent. When the stress in her voice tells you how sincere her need for $80 is.

Do you walk past a few people so everyone can see that you gave her the $80 she needs? This way everyone can recognize that you did something nice for her.

OR

Do you position the $80 in your pocket and as you walk past her you simply allow the money to appear to fallout of our pocket. Then pick up your pace as you quickly leave.

It is about the relationship you create with your-self that makes the difference.

Then it is the relationship that you make with others that seal your fate in light.

RULE #11 – SHARE THE LOVE YOU FEEL THROUGHOUT YOUR DAY TO DAY LIFE

QUESTIONS AND TIPS TO THINK ABOUT AS YOU READ RULE #11

Did you ever feel the love in a room when you enter it?

Did you ever feel the room light up when a person walks in and simply greets everyone in the room with a calm and peaceful smile?

Did you ever share the warmth of a handshake or simple friendly hug?

Can you let love flow through you, too someone, by just smiling as you introduce yourself?

RULE #11 – SHARE THE LOVE YOU FEEL THROUGHOUT YOUR LIFE WITH EVERYONE YOU MEET. MAKE SHARING LOVE YOUR PURPOSE IN LIFE

This is how you manifest love.

This whole process of creating a body, spirit and soul that is integrated as one being in love and light is all about bringing our thoughts, words and actions together in harmony with one another.

As we learn to live with an intention that is in sync with our actions we have achieved the first level of spiritual integration.

As our feelings, emotions and intentions align with one another through our thoughts, words and actions we have transformed our spirit into a light that shines bright.

When our thoughts and words integrate into our intention we have achieved the second level of integration.

When our thoughts, words and actions become sincere we have completed the first phase of integrating our spirit and soul into one being in the mind.

As we learn to live with a purpose in our life we begin to integrate the body and mind. As purpose fills our life our body and mind become more in rhythm with one another. As that which we create in spirit throughout our lives becomes centered on our purpose we are more completely integrating our body and mind. Now our personal essence is free to experience our life.

As our purpose grows into something that feels all-consuming as if this is what you were meant to do your spirit and souls purpose becomes your life's work or life's purpose.

When our spirit and soul are filled with darkness our essence appears to be very small as if hidden in all the darkness of our life. As the darkness fades and love grows in your life the essence of your spirit and soul begins to show itself. As you become sincere in your intentions and your life becomes filled with purpose the essence of who you are becomes a reality in your life.

When two people share a common purpose they live to accomplish something. This is one way in which manifestation works. When the spirit of two or more people combine to accomplish a common goal or purpose the spirit of their efforts manifests (or creates) the spirit of their efforts.

RULE #12 – BE PURPOSEFUL IN EVERYTHING YOU DO IN LIFE

QUESTIONS AND TIPS TO THINK ABOUT AS YOU READ RULE #12

Have you ever felt the over whelming feeling of being consumed by doing something?

Have you ever felt the spirit of a team of group of people that were working to save a life or accomplish a shared purpose?

Have you ever been consumed by something that you were trying to do?

How did it feel to be consumed by a project?

Were you able to hold on to the feeling of being filled with purpose for a long time?

Are you able to be consumed by your purpose when you are doing something alone but not when you work in a group?

RULE #12 – BE PURPOSEFUL IN EVERYTHING YOU DO IN LIFE

The spirit of working in a large group will manifest a much larger spirit than an individual person can manifest. Thousands of years ago, it was the spirit of large tribes and nations that manifested the gods that were referred to as the god of war, peace, love etc.

As we evolve into a greater light and higher consciousness it is only natural that love based purpose and consciousness will evolve. This is both an individual and collective evolution.

It is only natural that, as one person evolves others will follow.

This is how we evolve through creation and manifestation.

A love-based reality will bring with it sincerity. Sincerity will evolve into a purpose. A purpose will grow into being filled with purpose. Then a purposeful life will manifest the best possible realities in our lives.

This is how creation and evolution will eventually make this world a better place.

You do not have to strive to be purposeful, it will just happen as we evolve into it.

To be sincere in what you say think and do evolves from having a personal spirit strong enough to hold light. The stronger your spirit becomes the more sincere and purposeful you will be. I hope you can see how you feed off of that which you create in your spirit; in your life. This is how to create your reality.

After we create a purposeful reality in our lives, we will manifest a better world together.

Whether we are working to make the world a better place through a coven, at work, on a team or through the congregation of our church, when we all learn to agree and work together we will make this world a better place.

THE PROCESSES & REALITIES OF NATURE AND CREATION

In the beginning God created creation and creation created the realities of life and continues to create what we need from one generation to the next. Creation is the spirit and soul of creation; an extension of God. In order to accomplish the intention that existed when God (the Creator) created creation the spirit of nature and the spirit of creation had to exist. God created creation; then the spirit of creation created the spirit of nature. There are realities of nature and there are realities of creation that are similar in nature but very different as far as their roles in re-creating your spirit and soul. You transform (or re-create) your spirit from a hardened heart that is not capable of hearing the word of God, to a fertilized spirit capable of holding light this is higher vibrating spirit. This same process of transformation happens collectively as well as individually. As the individual and collective spirit(s) of mankind transform themselves the ambient spirit we manifest all around the world will change also.

AS STATED IN PART 1

In the physical we live, eat and breathe our realities based on time. Today's reality is a function of what we are going to do in the waking hours of the day. The reality we create is a function of what we did yesterday and want to do tomorrow. Our reality also is a function of our emotional health and well-being which is directly linked to our spiritual health and well-being. Spiritual health and well-being is a function of our spirit's strength or ability to hold light. When our spirit is consumed by light we will feel love. When it is consumed by darkness we will feel anger, hatred or rage. When we are not able to feel love at all there is an emotional block that exists within us that prevents us from being capable of feeling love. All the colors of the spectrum from white through red, orange, yellow, green, blue, violet, purple, all shades of gray and black have a specific vibration associated with them. Our spirit also has a vibration specific to it. We are capable of living with a spirit that is any or all of these energetic vibrations throughout our life. When our spirit is unhealthy it is too weak to hold the vibrations that are represented by these colors of the rainbow or white. An unhealthy spirit is not capable of holding these higher vibrating energies. Darker colors like gray and black are considered lower vibrating energies. Light and dark energies are polar opposites of one another and generate feelings within us that are also polar opposites; like love and anger comes from light and dark energies respectively. When our spirit is not capable of holding a positive vibration we are sealed away from feeling that love and the conscious awareness that comes with it. Since we react to our feelings we will naturally live with a reality that is created through anger or love depending on the health and well-being of our spirit. Anger becomes a driving force in our physical reality until we can create a meta-physical change in our spirit's reality.

In spirit our reality is a function of what our spirit and soul is or is not consumed by. A healthy spirit will be consumed by our Will to accomplish a goal or purpose. An unhealthy spirit might be consumed by the spirit of greed, lust or gluttony that motivates a person's actions and behaviors. If we are experiencing love at one moment in time our spirit will have a love-based experience. If we are experiencing anger our spirit will exist in that moment with a darkness that is a reflection of the anger that created it. If we are depressed our spirit will experience a lack of life as if it is asleep (this is often referred to as being dead to creation). When we have an unhealthy spirit we are not capable of experiencing our life with a certain range of thoughts, feelings and emotions. When we go from being happy go lucky one minute to being filled with anger, hatred or rage the next it may be because our spirit is not capable of holding the light needed to express our self in any other way. If we lose our ability to love we lose our ability to cope with a lot of situations through love and compassion. Without love in our lives our spirit is not capable of allowing us to express love to others. When someone says the words, "I just don't care" it will immediately create a spirit that just does not care.

A person whose spirit cannot experience love and light at all may not even be able to say the words, "I love you". This is our spirit and soul's reality. These are the reasons why it is important to think about our spiritual health and live to create a spiritually healthy life. With a spiritually healthy life our spirit can exist in our lives in such a way as to allow us to be consumed by the light and love of our spirit's reality every single moment of every single day.

A healthy spirit must be created and maintained by practicing forgiveness and allowing love to exist in your life.

These realities exist as processes and as realities in our personal life. These realities and processes help us to experience good and evil while learning to heal our spirit and soul. Creation creates what we need in order to accomplish the original intention that God had when creation was created. He created creation for us to learn about good and evil. Creation continues to create what we need as we continue this quest to find our light.

PROCESSES

Processes of creation <u>re-create</u> our spirit and soul.

Processes of creation allow us to <u>create</u> a better way of life for ourselves individually and collectively and that which we manifest in the ambient spirit of mankind.

Processes of creation allow us to <u>co-create</u> through the relationships in our day to day lives. This will make the world a better place.

<u>REALITIES IN OUR PHYSICAL LIVES CHANGE AS OUR SPIRITS AND SOULS CHANGE</u>

As our spirit and soul changes we will attract people into our lives that are of a similar spirit as we are.

As the love and light or our spirit and soul flow throughout our lives we will change from living with insincerity in our intentions to living with a greater purpose in our lives. In everything we say, think and do there is an intention that combines with an emotion and the essence of what is motivating us to act at that moment in time; when we create. When we say what we mean and we mean what we say we are aligning our intention and the words we speak that create the spirit of our words. As the emotions we commit to these words comes into alignment with our intention we create from a deeper part of the essence or our personal spirit. When we tell half-truths, deceive or manipulate others with our thoughts, words and actions we are creating through the insincere intentions of an unpure spirit. The power of an insincere creation is much weaker than when we create with a sincere intention that is aligned with our thoughts, words and actions. This has a big effect on our personal spirit as well as the spirit of the relationships we create through the spirit of our words.

A person that lives with a spirit that is not capable of holding light is not capable of creating this alignment between his or intention, feelings and thoughts, words and actions. This means they cannot create through the essence of their own personal spirit. This is why they create through the essence of the spirit of greed, lust or gluttony. It is the wants, needs, desires and cravings that are the essence of greed, lust and gluttony that motivate you to act and you create through them.

As our spirit and soul continues to develop we will feel a sense of purpose in our thoughts, words and actions. This is when our soul's purpose will then attract that which it needs into our lives. As we live with purpose our spirit becomes stronger and capable of processing a greater light. What that purpose needs in order to survive will come to you. Your purpose will attract to you what it needs as you create through it.

This is how attraction works as a reality in our lives – as a reality in creation.

Processes of Creation are a reality of Creation. Some of these processes that exist in creation are:

Forgiveness
Living with love
Maintaining the light or dark of your spirit
Perpetuity
Spiritual Nourishment

"Forgiveness" and "living with love" are both process of creation. Both are individual processes and are linked together to make one larger process. As you forgive a little some love and light will enter your life as you use this additional love to continue forgiving someone even more love and light will enter your life. As you use this additional love to continue forgiving someone even more love and light will enter your life. This cycle of forgiving and loving will continue until your spirit is healthy again. All throughout your life you will need to continue practicing forgiveness in order to maintain your light.

The spirit of that which you create takes on its own life. It will strive to perpetuate its existence. It lives through you by feeding you the thoughts and feelings that existed in you when you created it. When you respond to these thoughts and feelings by emoting more of them you are feeding this creation what it needs to nourish its own existence. This is also true of that which the collective spirit creates in the ambient spirit of the world.

These processes are important parts of the realities that influence the paths we walk on through the light and darkness of our soul's existence. We begin our existence in a spiritual reality that is filled with love and light. As time goes on we begin to lose that light and the path we walk becomes a journey into living with a spirit not capable of holding light. Then one day when we realize we have the inner strength to create a better life for ourselves we begin the quest to find our light. This quest is all about re-creating our spirit and soul as we create a better reality for ourselves and co-create a better world for others.

THE TWELVE SPIRITUAL REALITIES OF NATURE AND CREATION

1) A broken spirit
2) Losing your light – creating a seal
3) Living with a spirit that is no longer capable of holding light – hiding from the light. Living with an insincere intention – Your journey into an anger-based reality
4) Finding your essence - That something that is your commitment to transforming your spirit and changing your life - the prodigal son moment
5) The quest to find the light of day. Transforming the soil of your spirit into a spirit that is fertile enough to hold light.
6) The process of forgive and live with love - Creating your grail cup
7) The process of maintaining your light. The beginning of living with intention
8) Healer heal thy self
9) Growing your soul - living with a sincere intention completing your grail cup and beginning to fill it with love, light and intention that will eventually evolve into a life overflowing (over glowing) with purpose
10) Strengthening your spirit and souls connection by co-creating through relationships with others. Creating your spirit's new reality; a reality that is based on spiritually and emotionally healthy relationships.
    Adding strength to your grail cup by integrating your spirit with the spirit of others is the beginning of the process that fills your cup with the blood of life.
11) Living a purposeful life – A life filled with purpose. This further strengthens the bond between your spirit and soul. With a strong bond between your spirit and soul you fill your cup with the essence of who you are through your purpose.
    As you fill your cup through relationships – Your cup will runneth over as your life fills with a purpose to make the world a better place for all.
12) Becoming one in body, spirit and soul allows your personal essence to be present in your day-to-day life.

THE FIRST SPIRITUAL REALITY OF NATURE IS:

A BROKEN SPIRIT

When people live in hurtful environments it is only inevitable that their spirit will lose its ability to hold light. It takes a person with a very strong spirit and willpower to maintain his or her light when in a hurtful environment.

When a spirit is broken it cannot just simply be patched or mended – it must be broken down completely and re-created so it can be stronger than it was when it was first broken. The spirit has seven parts that it will be broken into and the soul has twelve parts. A spirit becomes weak when it loses its source of power which is wisdom. Wisdom brings with it love and acceptance. Acceptance is about accepting others for who they are and having no expectations of them. The polar opposite of accepting others for who they are is the need to be accepted by others. The need to be accepted by others is all about having expectations of others. Most people will never achieve or meet your expectations. Denial accompanies having expectations of others.

When we enter this world it is only natural that we will be completely dependent on others. This leads to having expectations that others will do for us. As these expectations grow (and they will because the forces of creation will encourage its growth) we will end up wanting and needing others to do more and more for us and this will lead to a dependence on others and what the world has to offer instead of our true source of love and light – the Kingdom of the Heavens and the Kingdom of God. Without love-based acceptance the spirit and soul's connection to the wisdom of God weakens as it leaves the kingdom of God. Without love and acceptance a person's spirit will not have the strength to continue to forgive others that create an environment around them that is hurtful.

Without the capability to forgive the spirit breaks and begins its journey into a darker state of mind. Before it can be rebuilt or re-created it must be totally broken and then rebuilt. A spirit breaks because for some reason there is a weakness that exists in it. We come into this world to have experiences that will help us to find this problem within our spirit and then mend it. It is not an easy process but it does work. It is a shame that we must hurt so much in order to find the source of our problems – but that is just the reality of life at this point in time.

This process of breaking down your personal spirit is about replacing the loves that naturally make you feel good about yourself with people and things. People and things are needed to make you feel and motivate you to act on these feelings. When we manipulate or deceive others through our words and actions we are reacting to a feeling and/or thoughts that motivates us to do what we do. When we are not sensitive enough to other people's feelings we hurt them without even realizing it. It is thoughts and feelings that tell us to manipulate or deceive others. When it feels right and our thoughts justify our actions it seems normal or even natural to do what we do. When we are feeling emotional or spiritual pains it can seem as if hurting others will make our pain go away. The pain does leave but only for a short time and then it comes back. Until we learn to get past the issues in our lives that created these problems we will continue on this path of destruction.

When a person's spirit and soul is whole it functions as one complete whole being in love based-consciousness. As the spirit and soul experience suffering the spirit and soul separate. As suffering grows stronger the spirit weakens as it is further broken into seven parts. These seven parts have a light and a dark reality to them. In the dark these seven components exist in the following seven realities that are the darker side of the kingdom of the heavens:

Wrath – fear, anger, hatred and rage are lower levels of the spirit or wrath. These are the base emotions associated with a person's intentions when living with a spirit not capable of holding light. <u>The essence of wrath is fear</u>. Peace of mind will come to you as you overcome this spirit that starts small and grows as it manifests into every aspect of your life. It will continue to control your life until you replace fear with confidence and peace in your spirit and life. The higher levels of this spiritual reality are ire, distain and wrath. When a person loses his or her compassion (love of those that wish you harm) fear and terror replace this love. When fear and terror become a reality in your life you learn to be afraid.

Greed – Wants and needs rule a person's life when you strive to replace the natural love that is lost when a person's spirit exists with anger. <u>The essence of greed is wants and needs</u>. Greed and its wants and needs serve you when your natural need to feel good does not allow you to just feel good. This inability to just feel good is the result of having lost your spirit's ability to hold light. A person with a healthy spirit will feel and express love of family and friends naturally. A person with an unhealthy spirit will express anger or the need to have something to make the anger go away in the same situation. When a person has overcome this reality he or she will have found pure love. With love of family and friends a person will find it easy to be grateful for what others do for you and to be generous in what you do for others. Being grateful and generous will help you to overcome the wants and needs of the essence of greed.

Lust – As the light in a person's spirit continues to grow dim, anger grows into hatred as greed grows into lust. Desires rule a person's life as you strive to replace the natural love that is lost when a person's spirit exists with hatred. Love of self is replaced by the desires of the spirit of lust. <u>The essence of lust is desires</u>. When a person lives with the desires of lust he or she learns to use people to contain their anger and hatred. On one hand people become the source of your hatred; on the other hand people are used to contain the anger and hatred that become the primary emotions that you feel day-to-day. You learn to use people to contain the anger you live with as you learn to share the anger you feel with others. As lust grows in your spirit you will learn to manipulate and deceive others in order to present your-self as the person you want others to think you are. You will also learn to deny your-self. Learning to be merciful towards others is a sign that you have learned to overcome the trappings of the spirit of lust as you regain your love of self.

Gluttony – As the light of a person's spirit is almost gone hatred grows into rage and lust evolves into gluttony. Cravings rule a person's life when you strive to replace the natural love that is lost when your personal spirit exists with rage. The essence of gluttony is cravings. Learning to be righteous and to strive to do what you know is the right thing to do in your life will begin to create the positive vibrations that are needed to re-create your spirit in light. To be righteous in your day to day life is a very strong reality. This very strong reality is what is needed to overcome the controlling nature of the cravings of gluttony. In order to overcome the cravings of gluttony you must hunger for righteousness.

SLIPPING INTO THE ABYSS

When a person loses the ability to:

1) love those that wish him harm (compassion)
2) love others (especially family and close and friends)
3) love your-self
4) to love God, nature and creation

you will lose all contact with the light side of the kingdom of the heavens. To lose your love and light is to lose the sensitivity to sense and feel your impact on others. When your spirit is filled with hatred and rage your mind will fill you with thoughts that encourage you to rationalize that the hurtful things you do to others is acceptable. When a person feels compelled to hurt others as if it is acceptable to do so; he is doing what he feels is the correct thing to do, so he will be accepted by others or by those that he views as being in his social group or gang. When a person acts in a hurtful way with an intention to hurt someone else he separates from love and light consciousness. This separation from God leads to living your life with a spirit and soul that creates through suffering, this is "living in the abyss".

To live with a spirit that suffers at this level is to exist in and create through three states of mind (sloth, pride and envy):

Sloth – A state of mind that has its foundation in depression and a feeling of total de-motivation. To have no life in your spirit is to be depressed. To have no life in your spirit is to have little or no desire to create in your day to day life. It is like your soul is asleep. This is when your spirit is dead to the love and light of creation. The essence of sloth is depression.

A person living with a slothful spirit will feel ire towards life. Part of the process of healing through this state of mind is to allow yourself to cry when you feel sad. To mourn your losses and allow yourself to feel sad is the first step in overcoming this state of mind. Mourning creates a vibration and rhythm in your spirit that does not exist when you deny the hurt that lies within your spirit. By crying you are cleansing your spirit of the feelings you denied yourself while accepting the depression of sloth in your spirit. Crying will begin the process of creating a space in your spirit that will allow you to have the vibration needed to bring life into your spirit and into your life again. This will help you to rebuild your spirit in such a way as to no longer live with depression.

Of course there is a lot more work to do to overcome depression than to just cry or mourn the losses that exist in your life. Most people that live with depression block out the memories and feelings that created the depression. These blocks allow you to deny the hurtful things that happened. When you overcome these blocks you will be able to mourn these memories and put life back into your spirit. Depression ends when you no longer live in denial and allow yourself to feel again.

Pride – To live with a spirit filled with pride is the only way to survive in this darker side of the heavens.

To live with pride is to accept responsibility for yourself and those that society says you are responsible for. It is not about acting on love but on a sense of duty or responsibility that defines the spirit and life style that exists in this level or an unhealthy spirit. You are motivated by the money you make, the status of your job title, how many toys you have, the type of car you drive, the neighborhood your home is in, etc. When a person is driven to make good grades in school, go to the best schools possible, so you can get the highest paying job, can live in the right neighborhood, have the most expensive homes and cars; you are trying to make your-self feel like you fit in where you need to fit in. Living without emotions means that you will naturally need these things to make you feel good about your-self and your life. Pride serves a very important part in the grand scheme of life. At this level of spiritual disintegration it would be very difficult to live for a person to live without having pride in people and things you own. The essence of pride is the need to make the world evolve around you and to be at the center of attention. In this state of mind a person needs constant positive feedback from others. Without positive feedback form others this person will not be able to contain the distain for life that fills his or her spirit. People can mask this reality from themselves in many ways.

Many people can have all the same things but not have the same motivator or sense of being driven to have them. When an engineer loves engineering and excels at engineering just because he loves engineering; he is working for a sense of purpose not for the status of money, homes and cars. This difference in motivator is the difference between creating your spirit in the dark (for status and money) or the light (a sense of purpose).

You can grow beyond this state of mind by practicing humility. To be meek and humble defines the spirit of a person that has successfully created a light spirit instead of a dark spirit. When a person has a darker spirit he or she has to let everyone know that he or she is successful. This allows a prideful spirit to vibrate in such a way as to make you feel good about yourself.

Envy – When you reach this level of darkness in your spirit you have reached the pit of the abyss. When a person feels envy he or she feels inadequate when compared to someone else. An envious spirit is defined by, the need to compare yourself to others and the need to have more in order to feel like you are as good as or better than others. It is this feeling of inadequacy that motivates your actions. When your spirit is so weak that you have fully separated yourself in body, spirit and soul you need to take from others in order to not feel so weak. This feeling of inadequacy will usually mask its-self as thoughts and feelings that make you feel as if you will gain more power over others if you act on these feelings. Another way these thoughts and feelings might mask themselves is to make you feel as if your power is threatened by someone else. When someone has what you think or perceive you need to maintain your power and sense of self you are experiencing envy. Here your spirit motivates you to intentionally hurt others in order to make your-self feel accepted or normal. A person is experiencing envy when he does not have the right things or enough things, status and position in his life; therefore he feels inadequate or less than good enough. The typical reaction to this feeling is to try to take from others that something they have that makes them feel inadequate. Taking from others is all you can do to try to feel good about yourself again. Some people try to use the fact that they have more than someone else to intentionally make another person feel inadequate. These people experience the worst kind of envy. To intentionally try to make someone feel this bad is only a reflection of the reality that this person is in the worst possible state of mind. This person that needs to make others feel bad is the kind of person we all need to avoid. These people feel no remorse for what they do to others and will even tell you they do not care about the hurt they are causing others. The real shame about this is that an envious person is feeling so little or nothing inside that they cannot help themselves.

The spirit of envy must always be something we recognize and reject it from our lives. It can be a very over powering feeling that is difficult to reject; it is a feeling and a spirit that we must strive to minimize or eliminate from our life, our spirit and our existence. When you realize you are poor in the spirit of envy you will know the re-creation of your spirit has begun.

With no possible way to fill your spirit with the good feelings that come with love and light all you have in life to make you feel good are things, status and people that you can use to replace the natural goodness of having light in your spirit.

There are also seven parts of a person's spirit that exist as polar opposites of these seven states of mind. These seven love-based states of mind have their essence in:

1) Being righteous
2) Caring, sharing and showing mercy towards others – Caring about your-self as much as others. This level of caring brings with it a sense of confidence and conviction that is committed to every thought, word and action in your day-to-day life.
3) Pure love - A pureness that just glows and shines with every word that is spoken. It is a feeling of pure joy that sparks your creations. This love comes from the kingdom of the heavens, through your spirit and creates the reality that is your life.
4) A sense of peace or peacefulness that comes from acceptance – Accepting yourself completely as well as accepting others for who they are with no expectations. When you feel like a peacekeeper you are building this fourth part of your spirit.

In these last three states of mind the fire of your soul has been lit and your power to create comes from the life that thrives in your spirit and soul.

5) A passion for creating a better way of life for your-self and for others is the polar opposite of the spirit of sloth.
6) A passion for making the world a better place is the opposite of the spirit of pride.
7) The wisdom of God comes through in your words and actions as you live without the negativity of envy. Living with the strongest connection to your spirit and soul as you express your-self as a complete and whole being of love, light and consciousness. As your spirit and soul become one in your mind your connection to God consciousness begins to grow as you begin to share God's message and Will on earth.

THE SECOND SPIRITUAL REALITY OF NATURE IS:

LOSING YOUR LIGHT - CREATING A SEAL

When a person's spirit is broken and forgiveness is not attainable the spirit and soul are sealed away from the love and light of God's creation – The light of the kingdom of the heavens.

The kingdom of the heavens is the source of all emotions and consciousness. There are two halves of the kingdom of the heavens that each contains the seven realities of the light and dark. The two halves are sometimes referred to as the dark of night and the light of day. There is also a part that exists to help us learn to live with our spirit as it changes. This transition area has two regions in it; one of lesser light and one of greater light. During this transition a person's spirit is either developing a seal as it journeys into its own darkness or releasing its seals as it begins its quest to find the light of day. These four parts of the heavens are linked to the four parts of a person's spirit that are the four loves (love of God, nature and creation, love of self, love of others and compassion).

When a person loses his capability to love he loses the power and strength needed to forgive those that wish him harm or have created an environment that is hurtful. When the pain and suffering of living, with the sensitivity that comes with emotions, becomes more than a person can bear he will give away his love. This begins the process of creating a seal. Living with love and in a hurtful environment can be more than a person can take; giving away the emotions that allow you to feel pain and suffering may feel like the only way to deal with this situation. Without love in your heart there is no light in your spirit and it is only a matter of time until you are no longer capable of forgiving those that wish you harm or have created an environment that is hurtful.

When a person is not capable of forgiving others the journey into darkness is complete and the seals that seal his spirit away from light begin to form. Fear, anger, hatred and rage enter your life and as you act on them these seals become complete. Acting on anger, hatred and rage creates the darkness in your spirit that limits you from hearing the word of God and from sensing love and light from others.

A seal is simply the darkness in your spirit that seals your spirit and soul away from love and light.

This gray area of the kingdom of the heavens allows your spirit to transition from light to dark and dark to light. During this transition you are learning to live in a different reality.

THE THIRD SPIRITUAL REALITY OF NATURE IS:

LIVING WITH A SPIRIT THAT IS NO LONGER CAPABLE OF HOLDING LIGHT – HIDING FROM THE LIGHT

LIVING WITH AN INSINCERE INTENTION

When living with a spirit that is not capable of holding light is a reality in which we strive to hide from the light that used to give us a natural feeling that made us feel good. It is like the true essence of our spirit hides from our consciousness and our spirit feels so bad that it just wants God to end its existence. This is the essence of how a person feels when their spirit is not capable of holding light. We have to either learn how to live in this state of mind or to heal our spirit.

To live in this state of mind is very challenging at first because you do not want to lie to people but at the same time it feels uncomfortable to be completely honest with them. You feel like you have very little and as if everyone is trying to take what you have; and if you are completely honest with others they will in some way use it against you. Quite often you will feel as if others will or hurt you if you let them know the truth about you. It is like if you let someone know how much money you have the price of something you want to buy might increase. The greedy nature of people with a dark spirit forces others with a dark spirit to live with the distrust they share with one another. You might feel very dependent on the things you have in your life as if you have to protect yourself and your family from the reality that you might lose them and your things. This is when people create negative realities in their life. When you believe that others will hurt them, you will treat others in a distrustful or hurtful manner; thereby creating the fear and the reality they feel. This is how a self-fulfilling prophecy works. As you believe something bad is going to happen you can manifest that something into your life.

This need to protect yourself, your things and your family can overpower your thoughts and the decisions you make throughout your day to day life. This fear makes it difficult for you to be totally honest with others and leads you to be very insincere with them.

This insincerity is a reflection of your lack of emotions. With emotions comes the need to be true to your feelings and this leads to being more sincere when you talk to people.

The more you feel uncomfortable sharing the complete truth about your life the less sincerity will come through in the spirit that you create as you interact with others.
Insincerity diminishes your power to create. When your intention, thoughts, words and actions are not in sync with one another your power to create is weakened. Along with this

misalignment between intention and thoughts, words and actions are lower vibrating and negative emotions that will further weaken your power to create.

Living with an insincere intention is a reality that exists with a darker spirit. Over time this will change. It is not like you are stuck with this reality forever. When your time comes you will find the inner strength to change.

THE FOURTH SPIRITUAL REALITY OF NATURE IS:

FINDING YOUR ESSENCE - THAT SOMETHING THAT IS YOUR COMMITMENT TO TRANSFORMING YOUR SPIRIT AND CHANGING YOUR LIFE

THE PRODIGAL SON

Finding that something, that oomph, that will charge your spirit with the commitment needed to transform your spirit and motivate you toward your quest to find the light of day.

The story of the Prodigal Son is about a young man that takes his father's endowment and leaves his family in search of fame and fortune. After a period of time he lost all his money and struggled to survive. Then one day he realizes he is sleeping in a pen with pigs. The most critical moment in a person's life is that moment in time when he accepts that he has made a mistake and begins his quest to return to his father. Sleeping with pigs is an important part of this story. Sleeping represents the spirit being asleep and the pigs are the un-pure spirits you associate with or are attracted too when in a darker state of mind.

The moral of this story is that we all get to that point in our lives when we stop rationalizing that we are living a righteous life. At this point we stop denying ourselves the truth about who we are, what our spirit is like and what we have created in our lives. This first moment of acceptance, begins the process of re-creation. At this moment our spirit becomes charged with a new reality; a new truth. This reality is one that gives us the drive that is needed to re-create our spirit and our lives. This quest is the search for what we must do to return our spirit to a state of mind that will allow us to find true joy in life. This joy in life comes to us naturally from the source of all love, light and consciousness that comes from the kingdom of the heavens. This joy replaces the need for things in our lives that will make us happy with an ever present feeling of peace. This new reality is one that allows us to feel happiness just because we can; there is no need to have people in our lives for the sole purpose of using them to make us feel good. We feel good just because we can.

To have a spirit that is weak is to not have the inner strength or will power to just be honest with our-self or others.

The most important point to take from this story is that we all take this path in life. It is not until we reach this point where we truly want to change that we are going to be able to change. To change requires that we do whatever is necessary to make our lives better. It is not the sort of thing that we can force into our lives by having an intention to change. It takes this moment of realization to create the acceptance of who you are and your commitment to change. Without both of these realities in your life you will not have the motivation that is needed to change.

It is at this moment of creation that you find your true essence, your God spark or spark of creation. Your journey into these darker realities ends as your quest to fill your spirit with light begins.

THE FIFTH SPIRITUAL REALITY OF NATURE IS:

THE QUEST TO FIND THE LIGHT OF DAY

TRANSFORMING THE SOIL OF YOUR SPIRIT INTO A SPIRIT THAT IS FERTILE ENOUGH TO HOLD LIGHT

This quest is about picking up your cross and carrying it. When you reach this point in your life there will be nothing more important to you than dealing with your issues in life. This quest to re-create your spirit and find your light will become the most important thing in your life. This commitment is necessary in order to find that which you seek while on this quest to create your grail cup.

When a person's spirit exists in the darkness of the abyss it is like living with a soil that is not capable of growing a spirit in light; not capable of finding your way into the light of God consciousness; not capable of doing what most people think of as right. A dark spirit is not capable of being righteous. A dark spirit is not capable of feeling love and many people with a spirit that is not capable of holding light cannot even say the word "Love" more or less let it flow through their thoughts, words and actions.

When in the deepest darkest part of this abyss, your heart is hardened because your spirit does not have what it needs to allow you to feel any other way. Trying to create through a positive intention while your spirit is not capable of holding light is like trying to plant a seed on a rock. The seed will not grow and will become food for birds. When the soil of your spirit is hard you cannot hear the word of God nor grow a soul that has a connection to God consciousness. With a hardened heart you might think you have a righteous intention and action; but your thoughts and feelings deceive you into believing this when in reality they are hurtful.

But with even the smallest intention to find your way into a better way of life you can create cracks in this rock that is your spirit. These cracks will allow the goodness of your thoughts, words and actions to try to grow like a seed that finds a little shade and moisture within the cracks that exist in the soil. Of course the soil of your spirit is not fertile enough to allow the spirit of your intentions to grow; but your spirit is becoming healthier.

It is like you are striving to find the right solutions to your problems but you are not quite capable of overcoming the thoughts and feelings that guide you. At this point in your spiritual development your thoughts and feelings guide you to continue to do hurtful things to others. It is like you do not have the sensitivity in your spirit to allow you to feel the effects of what you are doing to others. Without this sensitivity you do not know that you are hurting others through insensitive thoughts, words or actions and the insincerity of your intentions. But you are trying to find your way out; you just do not have the willpower to get there yet. Rest assured you will get there it is just a matter of time until you spirit becomes a soil that is fertile enough to bring light into your spirit and love into your heart.

When you learn to forgive others for the hurtful things they have done to you the process of fertilizing your soil begins. The more you forgive others the more forgiveness will be created in your spirit. The more sincere your intention and the more love you commit to it the greater the forgiveness you will create in your spirit. Forgiving others for what they did to you and forgiving your-self for what you did to others are two ways that you will be able to create forgiveness in your spirit and begin to fertilize the soil that is your spirit. The most important part of this process is that you must be sincere and you must commit love to that which you wish to create - Forgiveness.

As you fertilize the soil of your spirit, you become more sensitive to others and begin to realize that your actions do affect others in a way you were not previously aware of. Your relationships with others will begin to change as you learn to create a better way of life for yourself and with others. Many people that fertilize their spirit will begin to recognize that their friends still do hurtful things to others; this will motivate you to attract new friends into their life. This commitment to you and to your life will help to speed up the transformation of your spirit. By acting in such a way as to make your spirit and its health a priority in your life will accelerate your transformation. It is like the seeds you plant with others will now have a chance to grow as your power to create better relationships will grow. The first relationship is your relationship with your-self; with your spirit.

It is not like you have completely cleansed your spirit or fertilized it in such a way as to only grow healthy relationships. You still have some work to do as you learn to always do the right thing (to be righteous). Becoming righteous in your thoughts, words and actions is the last part of cleansing and fertilizing your spirit. As you live with a spirit at this first level of healing you have good intentions but do not always say and do the right things towards others. It is like you have to leave all the things you learned while living in a darker state of mind behind you; this is not always easy nor does it happen overnight. You have to maintain your commitment to this change and to your quest to find your light in order to grow beyond the thorns of your thoughts, words and actions. As you continue to practice forgiving yourself and others for the hurtful things you experienced throughout your life you will continue to create a more fertile spirit and you will become more sensitive to your impact on others. It is like a reward to become more sensitive to how other people feel instead of being sensitive to the words and actions of others. To no longer be hurt by the words or actions of others is the first benefit that you feel as you create your grail cup.

When you care deeply about others and thrive on the relationships you create with them you will want to share who you are with them. The seeds you plant will grow deep roots in the relationships you create. When you have reached the point in this process of creation you will begin to produce relationships just like a pepper plant will produce an abundance of peppers or a field of wheat will produce grains for you to use to make bread. Now you are ready to live a life that is fruitful. It becomes fruitful because the quality of the relationships and the spirit of those relationships will feed your spirit, your soul and others that are connected to your spirit. These relationships and how they feed your spirit becomes the fruit of your labors.

As your spirit begins its evolution out of the dark of night you are experiencing the spirit of nature's role in your spiritual evolution.

As your spirit evolves into creating healthier relationships you will experience the spirit of creations role in your spiritual evolution.

THE SIXTH SPIRITUAL REALITY OF NATURE IS:

THE PROCESS OF FORGIVE AND LIVE WITH LOVE

CREATING YOUR GRAIL CUP

The process of Forgive and Live with Love is a process of creation; it is a reality that evolved from God's original intention.

Forgiveness is a process and living with love is a process. They are two separate processes that are intricately linked to each other. As they work together to transform your spirit into a stronger healthier existence you will change the reality that is your life.

Forgiving someone or seeking forgiveness from others for things you did in the past is only the first step in re-creating your spirit. When forgiving someone you must really want to forgive them. It is the sincerity on your intention and the love that flows with it that will create a forgiving spirit.

The second step is to let your spirit fill with light. Forgiveness cleanses your spirit and makes it capable of holding light; you still have to allow it flow from your spirit into your heart.

The third step is to let your spirit fill you with love. It is normal to resist allowing these emotions to flow into your life. When people lose emotions it is usually because they lived in an environment or had an experience that made it too difficult to live with them. The pain and suffering of living with them is what motivates people to give them away. So to accept emotions back into your life may be more challenging than you first think. At this step you learn to create a better life for your-self. As people live with light in their spirit and love in their hearts we have the opportunity to make this world a better place.

The fourth step is that you have to share it with others. At this step you learn to co-create a better life through relationships with others. This is how we make the world a better place for all. Making the world a better place begins with loving one another. Accepting others for who they are and life for what it is will grow into a sense of peace in your life. As peace of mind enters your spirit, peace on earth will manifest into your life and the lives of others that are close to you.

These steps happen naturally as you become more sensitive to the feelings of others. This sensitivity to others will solidify the changes you have made in your spirit up to this point. By solidifying these changes through love and the sensitivity that is now a part of your life you will make it easier for you to love others even those that wish you harm.

The following explains the cycle of filling your cup with love through forgiveness.

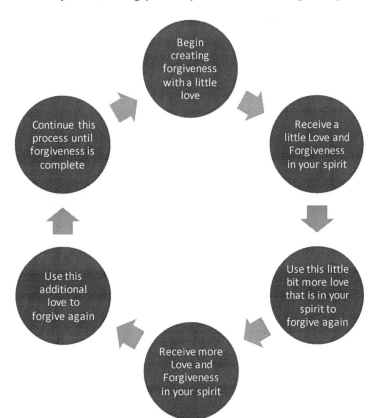

When you begin the process of forgiveness you will usually feel compelled to forgive others for the hurtful things they did to create suffering in your life. You lived with this suffering because of hurtful things that were done to you. When you were unable to forgive those that hurt you it was only natural that you would then treat others in the same way that you were treated. It is a way of feeling normal or, as if, since this is the way you were treated it is only right that you should treat others the same way that you were treated. When you meet the same people that mistreated you, it is only normal that you will intentionally treat them the way they treated you, as if to share your pain with them. No matter how hard you try you cannot give it back to them and you cannot change your reality by sharing these old negative feelings with others.

Forgiving those that hurt you will only cleanse your spirit of the darkness that was created when you were unable to forgive their hurtful behaviors. Cleansing your spirit is like changing its color from black to gray. When you forgive someone your spirit is becoming capable of being fertilized like making cracks in the hardened soil of your spirit.

Then as time goes on you will have moments of intense emotions. As light flows into the cups of your spirit it will seem like these cups of light will overflow. When your spirit overflows with light you will feel love. When they overflow you will suddenly feel very good about yourself and about life again. It is only natural that you will feel uncomfortable at first.

To feel these emotions after not feeling them for so long might make you want to push them away. Remember, in the past when you had these feelings and lived in a hurtful environment you naturally wanted to <u>not</u> feel them. These feelings hurt when you felt them and this is why most people will, at first, resist feeling them again. After a series of moments when you feel this overwhelming love in your heart you will naturally want to feel it again. When you get to this point you will become so committed to loving that you will give up anything and everything in your life so you can continue to feel this way.

The last step in this process of loving is to share these feelings with others throughout your day to day life. The challenge is that you suddenly feel so good that you may not want to share them with others. You still have to adjust to the fact that you are not going to lose them. The key to feeling a greater depth of love is to share them with others. The simple act of caring about and sharing love with others will only make your spirit stronger; thereby allowing you to process more light and love through you. The more you share it the more you will feel like sharing it until your spirit is full. Now you have created a healthy spirit. This is the completion of the first part of your quest to find your love and light.

You have now created a grail cup. Your spirit in light is your grail cup. At this point in your healing process you have shaped your grail cup and made it capable of holding light. Now you have to make it stronger. It will become stronger as you continue to live with sincerity and purpose in your life.

This is how you repent and then overcome the lifestyle you lived while your spirit was not capable of holding light.

THE SEVENTH REALITY OF CREATION IS:

THE PROCESS OF MAINTAINING YOUR LIGHT

THE BEGINNING OF LIVING WITH INTENTION

At this point in your quest you have found your grail cup and have learned how to fill it. As you have learned to fill the four parts of your spirit with light you have found the seven cups that are you, that are your spirit. Now you have to learn to maintain the light in your spirit and love in your life.

There are four loves that represent your four cups, they are:

Love of God, Nature and Creation
Love of Self
Love of others (especially family and close friends)
Compassion – Love for those that wish you harm

These four loves live outside of your body and a lot of people think of this as their aura or countenance.

The last three parts of your spirit exist inside of your body and connect your spirit to your soul. As love creates the cups and the strength of these cups is a function of the depth of your love; what you fill your cups with is just as important as the love that creates them. You fill your cups with your purpose in life. To begin filling your cup with purpose you have to first learn to live with intention and to have a sincere intention in everything you do in life. This will make the cup stronger and you will begin to fill it with your life's purpose. This is where the link between your spirit and soul begin to form.

When a person lives with a spirit that cannot hold light he or she will naturally not be sincere in their intentions in life. People without light in their spirit live with fear and one of the greatest fears is to share. Sharing what a person has, can be a very uncomfortable reality. With a dark spirit, the feeling of giving is often similar to the feeling of losing something. So living with a sincere intention is a challenge that most cannot overcome until they cleanse their spirit.

When a person lives with light in their spirit it is only natural that they will learn to live with intention. They say what they mean and mean what they say as they go about their day to day lives. Learning to trust that being open and honest will not hurt, is a big step in learning to continue to love others in your life. This act of being true to yourself is important because it is the beginning of trusting your-self and this is when you begin to grow your light-based soul. As you fill your cup with intention you are making your cup stronger (your spirit brighter). Your soul is the consciousness that will eventually feed you what you need to know in order to maintain the strength of your spirit. Until you accept your light-based spirit and learn to live with it in the right way, your soul will not grow. Living with an intention to do the right thing in life and do the right thing as it relates to others is the beginning of the process of accepting your spirit, its light and its love.

When you live with a spirit that is in transition from dark to light it is only natural to want to use your spirit to make your life easier. You will want to use your power to create – to create or manifest things in your life that will make your life easier. Here in this state of transition you still have wants, needs and desires in your spirit and it is only natural to still believe that they are what you need to make you happy or what you need to live your life. It is as if you feel that these things have to be there for you so you can continue your quest to create your grail cup. They are not required and you will realize this as your spirit continues to grow and your cup is complete.

You will know that your spiritual cup is healthy when you realize that all you need is to be more true to your-self, sincere with others and fill your life with purpose. This will naturally guide you to be more trusting of others; then you will feel comfortable being sincere in your intentions; thereby filling your cup. When your cup is filled with the love and light of living with purpose and sincerity you will naturally want to share it with others – this is when you share your love with others by allowing them to drink your spirit (sometimes referred to as blood of life) from the cup of your love. When you share a common purpose with others you are combining or joining your spirit with theirs. As these spirits join into a group of people it like is drinking from each other's cups. This is what spiritual nourishment is all about. Feeding off of each other's purpose will create an even stronger spirit in you. With this stronger spirit in you and the others involved with this collective purpose, the group will create the cup of the spirit of their collective purpose. As this collective spirit grows into a love-based, purpose filled consciousness – this group of people will experience the, "We Are Us" consciousness.

THE EIGHTH SPIRITUAL REALITY OF CREATION IS:

HEALER HEAL THY SELF

Let's recap for a minute:

Your spirit is your connection to feelings.
Your soul is your connection to the conscious awareness that enters your consciousness as the result of where your spirit exists in the kingdom of the heavens (how much love and light or lack of love and light exists in your and your spirit) at any point in time.

You feel feelings and express emotions.
Your consciousness is a state of knowing what you need to know when you need to know it. Your intention guides your spirit into this place in the heavens (dark or light) and then your soul follows.

Your feelings are a function of your intention at any moment in time. Your thoughts are a function of where your intention guides your spirit and soul, and when you act on a thought or feeling you create a spiritual reality in your life. This reality is a function of the essence of that which motivated you to have the intention and the emotion that accompanies the thoughts, words and actions you use to create this spiritual reality in your personal spirit.

There are more sources from which you receive thoughts and feelings but for now let's just focus on the above.

When a person lives in a darker state of mind he or she will only be capable of processing the same feelings they feel into the spirit they create. If you are not capable of feeling deep love for others you are not capable of creating love of others. A person who feels only anger throughout his or her life will only be able to feed more anger into the spirit of his or her creations; therefore lives with a spirit that is sealed away from light-based consciousness. Quite often people struggle to create better relationships with others, especially family. People eventually get to the point where they just can't seem to create something positive through these relationships. These positive things they need to create are more about healthy relationships not the manipulative realities that they usually end up with. In the end it is because they do not have the right intention or emotional capacity to create the changes they long to make in their lives. Emotional capacity is also a function of the collective spirit of mankind. Today the collective spirit has just started to enter the gray transition area of the heavens.

Struggles grow into conflicts and conflict grows into fights because those involved in these relationships are feeding off of the conflict. Without the emotional tool kit needed to create a change you can only perpetuate these relationships. Until a person begins the process of re-creating his or her spirit and achieves the results defined in the process of forgiveness the spirit will continue to feed off the same conflict that has existed throughout your life.

Creation creates through your true intention; by what your true intention guides your spirit and soul to do. You can tell others that you have a great and perfect intention all day long but when you keep having the same problems from one day to the next you are probably just fooling yourself and others. You are probably creating from a different intention than the one you have tried to convince yourself that you are creating through. Remember God (Creation) knows what is truly in your heart. You will create through that which is truly in your heart. The reality you create throughout your life is a reflection of that which you have created through in the past. As you learn to heal your-self you will learn to have one single intention with everything you do. As your intention grows into a sincere intention you will see the results you are striving to achieve; or be able to accept that your hearts intention is not where it should be in order to achieve it. Most people will find that their spirit is not as clean as they thought it was and they just are not capable of achieving the emotions needed to create the reality they desire. When you realize your intention is not where it should be and your emotional limitations are interfering with what you want to create you have achieved the moment of realization that comes with the spark needed to re-create your spirit and soul. Now your quest to find your light has begun.

When a person lives in a lighter state of mind he or she will have the capability to feel light or dark in their lives and to have access to conscious thoughts that he or she can control. This person with a lighter spirit is capable of choosing to feel one feeling or having one thought and be able to choose to emote and create through the same thoughts and feelings or to change the reality that exists in his or her personal spirit by consciously feeding their spirit and soul a different thought and feeling. This is how we heal our-self, our personal spirit and soul. When a person has created enough light in his or her own spirit it is only natural to want to use it to make your own personal spirit better. You will want to change your reality in life; you will learn that you have the power to do so. By using your ability to transform your thoughts and feelings from being negative and anger-based to positive and love-based your reality will change.

It is only natural that the gap between your personal intention and your spoken intention will shrink. As this gap shrinks, your spirit and soul become healthier and your essence becomes a part of your life. It is as if your essence is no longer hidden from you.

Please remember this can only happen after you have re-created your spirit by making it capable of holding light. When a person lives in a darker reality their spirit is not strong enough to do the things a lighter spirit is capable of doing.

If a person has a conflict with a neighbor and a short time later feels the spirit of that conflict coming into his life; at first he may just feed the spirit of the conflict more of the same feeling he received from it. If you feed it anger it will continue to live. When you become aware that you are feeding it you can then make the conscious decision to change it. The next time he receives the same feeling from this past event he might choose to no longer accept that darker anger-based feeling and choose to feed it a more positive love-based feeling. This will change the spirit of that event. This is a reality that only exists if he has the capability to emote love. If his spirit is filled with anger and his soul is sealed away from the light – this person may not be capable of emoting love or simply allowing light to flow through you.

As you learn to feed your spirit and soul what it needs to continue on this quest to create and fill your cup with love and light you will find that your work has only just begun. Now that you have created forgiveness in your spirit, your power to forgive your-self and others and to love deeply is a part of a new reality in your life. With this powerful feeling of love in your life you will naturally want to experience more of it. Your spiritual creations from your past will still exist in your spirit even after you have completed the process of forgiveness. This is why you will need to continue the process of healing your-self by consciously feeding your spirit and your soul what it needs to create a new reality that is only one of love and light. You have to transform all the things you created in your spirit while living in a darker state of mind.

This will take time – perhaps even a lifetime or two but it is worth it as you bring a greater love and a greater sense of peace into your mind, into your reality in life and into the world.

THE NINTH SPIRITUAL REALITY OF CREATION IS:

GROWING YOUR SOUL

LIVING WITH A SINCERE INTENTION

COMPLETING YOUR GRAIL CUP AND BEGINNING TO FILL IT WITH LOVE, LIGHT AND INTENTION THAT WILL EVENTUALLY EVOLVE INTO A LIFE OVERFLOWING (OVER GLOWING) WITH PURPOSE

As a person learns to live with intention in everything he or she does, it is only normal to grow more and more sincere as to your intention in everything you do.
To be sincere and to not even think about stretching the truth or deceiving someone else with your words is when this ninth reality creates a permanent bond or connection between your spirit and soul.

As you fertilized your spirit with the higher vibrations of light and love you created the environment through which your soul can grow. It is only natural that your personal soul will now grow in such a way as to allow you to live a life that will be spiritually healthy and productive.

It is the sincerity of your intention that will let your soul begin to connect you to the consciousness that is the light side of the heavens.

Your spirit feeds you feelings and your soul feeds you thoughts this makes you consciously aware of your reality in life.

In general terms there are two types of thoughts that your soul feeds you:

1) Thoughts that help you <u>accomplish</u> your intentions or purpose in life.
2) Thoughts that help you <u>maintain</u> the light or dark of the spirit of your intentions and purpose(s) throughout your life.

In that moment of creation when you have an intention that is hurtful in nature, your spirit responds to your intention and you will feel the darkness (anger or fear) of it. Your soul feeds you what you need to know it in order to make your intention a reality in your life. Others may also feel the spirit of your intention. When your intention is sincere others will feel the sincerity and it may even make them feel more comfortable with you. In this way your thoughts, words or actions and feelings help you accomplish your intention.

In your day-to-day life your soul also feeds you what you need to know so you can maintain the overall dark or light of your spirit (this is your personal state of nature). If you have a love-based state of nature your spirit will feed off the seven spirits of the light side of the heavens. This light flows through your spirit and then feeds you feelings, which will encourage you to continue on your quest to live in and find more love and light. As you feed off these feelings your soul is working to maintain your light and love. Your soul is feeding you thoughts and awareness of what you need to know in order to maintain this level of light. Your soul will feed you thoughts and encourage you to act in such a way as to maintain and grow the light in your spirit. When you are happy, laughing and full of love your soul will feed you the thoughts what you need in order to help you maintain a loving reality in your life. When you are unhappy, sad and angry your soul will feed you what you need to know in order to maintain this anger based reality. It is up to you to choose to stay in an anger based reality or to not act on the thoughts your soul feeds you. When you wait until you are in a better mood before making difficult decisions you will be able to maintain a better light in your spirit.

The kingdom of the heavens is like having a range of feelings and thoughts that make you who you are. Within this range there can be only fear and anger-based thoughts and feelings (dark), love plus anger-based thoughts and feelings (gray) or only love-based thoughts and feelings (light). Within this range of thoughts and feelings, you live off of and feed your-self through these thoughts and feelings. Your behaviors and lifestyle become second nature to you. Remember the nature of your being can be either light or dark. You live and exist in a sort of harmony within yourself until you decide to make a change to this harmony. This is when you begin the process of change. This process of change begins because you realize there is a better way to live. This can be because you are in a very dark state of mind and want to find the light or because you live in the light and want to find more love in your life as you grow into a bright light.

As you live in your state of nature you may find these nagging thoughts that seem to bring you down and not be sure where they are coming from. They may come from spiritual creations you created in your spirit, in the past. Spiritual creations live and exist in all of our spirits and may affect your day-to-day life in such a way as to prevent you from feeling the love and light you want to live with. These spiritual creations were a part of the harmony that existed in your past when your state of nature was not the same as it is today. Now these spiritual creations or children that were a part of your past harmony are creating disharmony. Disharmony exists simply because you have changed your state of mind (the intention that is the foundation of your current state of mind); therefore your state of nature has changed and you are now motivated to grow beyond your past intentions. Your spirit and soul will now have what is needed to re-create them and to integrate them into your new state of nature as you shift your consciousness into a brighter light. The phrase overcoming the issues from your past is about growing beyond the nature of your state of mind so you can experience life in a new reality.

You re-create these past intentions as you become more aware of the thoughts and feelings that you have been feeding off of and when you feel a feeling or receive a thought that is not going to help you on your path; then you feed them the thoughts that you want them to feed off. The most important part of this process of re-creation is to act on these feelings and thoughts in a different way than they are trying to motivate you to act. This is why it is so important to always strive to do the right thing in your life. We all know right from wrong and it is these thoughts and feelings that motivate us to choose one or the other. From our choices we will create our spirit and the nature of who we are.

For example:

If you have always hated a family member – say a brother. You will be used to having thoughts and feelings that will feed that anger. As you go through the process of "Forgive and live with love" your intention will be to change your relationship. Just because you have an intention to change does not mean that all the past anger and its creations will just go away.

YOU have to change them.
YOU have to start to act differently in order to create the reality you desire. YOU have to begin to accept and try to remember the good times and to allow those good times to enter your thoughts.
YOU have to send positive thoughts to him.
YOU have to call him and talk to him and allow your feelings to change as they flow out of your mouth with every word you speak.
YOU have to create this new reality as you overcome the power of the reality that was created in the past.

THE TENTH SPIRITUAL REALITY OF CREATION IS:

STRENGTHENING YOUR SPIRIT AND SOULS CONNECTION BY CO-CREATING THROUGH RELATIONSHIPS WITH OTHERS – THE COLLECTIVE SPIRIT OF MANKIND AND HOW IT WORKS

CREATING YOUR SPIRIT'S NEW REALITY; A REALITY THAT IS BASED ON SPIRITUALLY AND EMOTIONALLY HEALTHY RELATIONSHIPS.

ADDING STRENGTH TO YOUR GRAIL CUP BY INTEGRATING YOUR SPIRIT WITH THE SPIRIT OF OTHERS IS THE BEGINNING OF THE PROCESS THAT FILLS YOUR CUP WITH THE BLOOD OF LIFE WHILE SIMULTANEOUSLY BEGINS CREATING THE COLLECTIVE SPIRIT OF MANKIND (OUR GRAIL CUP)

As a person's spirit becomes stronger it will continue to not only hold more light but hold a more pure light. It is the combination of more light and the pureness of the light a person creates that will determine the quality of love that will flow through a person's thoughts, words and actions. This quality is often thought of as the brightness of your spirit.

You grow a bright spirit through your relationships with others. It is a must that you begin to develop sincere, purposeful relationships with other people so you can continue to add strength to your spirit; to your grail cup.

It is very natural that you will grow through these steps of having a positive intention that becomes more sincere and then having a purpose in life. As these things happen your reality in life will change it will shift in to a better place. As your spirit begins to shine people will start to treat you with more respect. Others that have walked this same path will recognize the sincerity in your voice and feel the love in your spirit and, naturally, want to get to know you better. As you build relationships with others you will learn to feel more comfortable talking about yourself and listening to what others have to say.

With a spirit that cannot hold light a person is more self-centered and insincere, this makes it difficult to truly listen to what others have to say or to clearly hear and understand the word of God that comes from your inner voice. A person at this lower level of spiritual development hears a person's words but does not feel the spirit of their words; instead your mind motivates you to think about what you are going to say next. It becomes more important to think about how to respond to a person than it is to feel the spirit of his or her intention. This weaker spirit tries to feed itself through the other person's words and will strive to prevent you from feeling anything positive that might come from that person. Your spirit will act as a filter to prevent you from feeling the loving intention that comes from someone else. This is because, you feel and hear what your spirit allows you to feel and hear in order to perpetuate its-self. Some people become very sensitive to what others say to them and get their feelings hurt because they are not able to sense the true intention of another person's words or actions. After feeding off of this kind of sensitivity a person learns to live with the sadness within his or her spirit. This is one of the most challenging realities to overcome.

When a person grows a light spirit he or she will naturally sense and feel the spirit of another person's words more clearly. This will create relationships that are more fruitful. The spirit that grows from a love-based relationship is the fruits of your labor. The tastiness of the fruit is the quality of love and sincerity that is created by two people.

High quality relationships will create a stronger spirit that will allow your spirit to hold more light and a stronger body that can process more love through you. This is how to fill your grail cups with the spirit of your relationships.

As you live a life filled with purpose and create relationships that are filled with love and light your grail cup will over flow (over glow) as you live with the joy of just feeling good about your life.

Now, you should be able to see how living with a sincere intention will just naturally grow into a life filled with purpose. This is how your life will change as a new reality is created because you made it happen. The only way a person with a lot of anger in his or her life can change an anger-based reality is to forgive those that hurt you and those that you might have hurt throughout your life.

It is the process of loving others that will integrate your relationships and your purpose in life as your grail cup (your spirit) evolves into a higher vibration, a brighter light that glows with every thought, word or action in your day-to-day life.

As you live a life filled with purpose and acceptance your love becomes unconditional. Unconditional love transforms the four loves that are four parts of your spirit into one large light that is now your spirit, your grail cup.

HOW THE COLLECTIVE SPIRIT OF MANKIND WORKS WITHIN THESE RELATIONSHIPS

The collective spirit of mankind is made up of several layers:

Individuals
Families
Communities
Cities
Nations

The world is filled with all of the above. This is what the prophecy Revelations refers to as multitudes.

An individual is born into a family and the bright light of that child is consumed by the spirit of the household. The family's spirit is consumed by the spirit of the neighborhood or community it lives in. The community's spirit is consumed by the city and the city's spirit is consumed by the nation it is a part of. All the nations of the world make up the collective spirit of mankind.

A generation of children enter the world every 20- 22 years. This generation of children comes with a higher vibration of love and light in their spirit and a purpose to change the world completely. This generation of children will be consumed by the lifestyle created by previous generations. Families and communities teach these children how to live in the world that was created by previous generations. As these children grow through their teen years they are beginning to come into the spirit they will collectively live with for most of their life. This is a part of the collective spirit that will have the greatest impact on them. They will learn to grow beyond the issues of their childhood, forgive and love as they create a higher vibrating collective spirit of mankind.

There are 3½ generations that exist in any one lifetime. These lifetimes evolve through a set of purposes. These lifelong purposes are all linked together with an intention that comes from the collective spirit of the previous lifetime. Each and every lifetime is filled with people that pray and have deep rooted feelings about what they deeply believe will make this world a better place. The spirit of these prayers comes together to create the purpose(s) of future lifetimes and generations within these lifetimes. This is how the world (this is how we) continues to change and make our lives better lifetime after lifetime and generation after generation.

SUMMARY OF CREATING AND FILLING YOUR GRAIL CUP UP TO THIS POINT

You create your cup so it can hold the light of love and forgiveness.

Your cup takes shape and gets its initial strength as your intention in life becomes stronger.

With a stronger commitment to living with purpose and healthier relationships your cup becomes capable of holding a bright light.

As your intention evolves into a life filled with acceptance, unconditional love and purpose, the four loves of your spirit transform into your grail cup.

As you build relationships that have a greater sense of purpose you begin to fill this cup with the love that is shared between you and those that you connect with.

Building relationships that are purposeful will create the collective spirit of mankind's collective cup.

Then as you grow your spirit and soul through deeper felt feelings and emotions your life will grow into a greater sense of purpose; your cup begins to fill with the essence of the spirit of your purpose as the blood of life flows into and out of your cup.

THE ELEVENTH SPIRITUAL REALITY OF CREATION IS:

LIVING A PURPOSEFUL LIFE – A LIFE FILLED WITH PURPOSE

THIS FURTHER STRENGTHENS THE BOND BETWEEN YOUR SPIRIT AND SOUL AS YOU FILL YOUR CUP WITH THE ESSENCE OF YOUR PURPOSE

AS YOU FILL YOUR CUP THROUGH RELATIONSHIPS – YOUR CUP WILL RUNNETH OVER AS YOUR LIFE FILLS WITH A PURPOSE TO MAKE THE WORLD A BETTER PLACE FOR ALL

As your life becomes filled with this bright light you will feel like you can make the world a better place. You will naturally become comfortable with a heightened level of sincerity in your intention as you make the world a better place. It is as if you will feel very comfortable in your own skin, as if doing anything else would just not work and make you feel very out of place. At this point you have completely reversed the polarity of your spirit and soul and naturally feel compelled to live with a greater purpose in your life. Your spirit and soul will naturally draw you towards this greater purpose. As you feel the need to make a difference in the world; you will naturally act on feelings that motivate you to do something that you feel is of greater importance. As you continue to act on these feelings your spirit and soul will grow stronger and more in rhythm with one another. It is like you are consumed by a need to do what you are doing. You will not feel as if you are in control or out of control; just a feeling of purpose.

As your spirit and life becomes filled with purpose you are healing your spirit and soul in such a way as to bring them together in a much stronger way. Your body, spirit and soul are attracted to one another by the process of forgiveness and the love that accompanies it; then your body, spirit and soul bond together as one as you become more sincere and purposeful; then as your build higher quality relationships with others a spiritual bond is created between those that share a passion for a common purpose.

Thus far you have picked up and carried your cross, recreated your spirit and soul as you have created your grail cup and your cup is overflowing with the love and light of a life filled with purpose.

Earlier in this book we talked about the separation of the spirit and the soul. It is when your life is filled with purpose that your spirit and soul are beginning to come together as one again. You will feel a sense of rhythm as you feel the bright light of your purpose and then act on your feelings with a sense of confidence that you have never felt before. This confidence is about caring so much about others that you have no concern as to what others might think or say about you. It is common for your words to contain a lot of wisdom in them as the sincerity of who you are grows through everything you say, think and do in your life. Some people think of this as the marriage of the spirit and soul.

Becoming one with the intention(s), purpose, feelings and emotions of every thought, word and action will transform your spirit and soul into one being in love, light and consciousness.

Until now you have been living with a spirit that existed in the collective spirit and soul of mankind. People that are able to grow their spirit and soul beyond the collective spirit of mankind are now capable of impacting the collective spirit in a much greater way. This level of bright light that flows and glows through your thoughts, words and actions is the most incredible feeling you will ever experience. As you grow beyond the level that all others have been capable of evolving into, you will set the standard for all others to follow. At this point in your spiritual development you are creating the path into this higher light that others will be able to follow. Those that are closest to you will sense and feel a change within them and then be drawn to follow your lead. This is when your power to create becomes very strong. It becomes stronger because you have no wants or needs, desires or cravings for anything for yourself – you will merely allow whatever your purpose needs, to enter your life. When you no longer use your spirit to manifest what you want and need you have allowed your spirit to grow to this much brighter level of light. Now you merely allow the spirit of your purpose to manifest in your life and throughout the world. You will gain a greater awareness of your-self, your purpose and all the spirit that surrounds you. This is the beginning of becoming one in body, spirit and soul.

THE TWELFTH SPIRITUAL REALITY OF CREATION IS:

BECOMING ONE IN BODY, SPIRIT AND SOUL

As your body, spirit and soul develop in such a way as to feed one another and to feed off of one another; your body, spirit and soul are now ready to become one being in love, light and consciousness.

Your soul will feed you the thoughts, words and actions needed to create what your spirit needs in order to maintain its spiritual health and well-being. Your soul will also feed you what you need to know in order to attract that which your body needs to live.

Your spirit will feed you what you need to motivate you to act in rhythm with the conscious thoughts that come from your soul. Your spirit will also feed you the feelings that you need in order to gage the depth of light associated with your intentions and purpose.

As you act on the thoughts and feelings of your soul and spirit you will create a life and an environment that will allow your grail cup to become one. With a healthy grail cup your soul merges with your spirit and you live to feed your spirit and soul while simultaneously feeding off of them. Now, your quest to transform your body, spirit and soul is complete as you will no longer have a need to exist in the kingdom of the heavens and you are resurrected as a being in love, light and consciousness. This is when you enter the kingdom of the God as a being of love, light and consciousness where you live and exist with balance and harmony within your-self. You will now have a heightened sense of pure consciousness in your existence.

Your spirit and soul work in rhythm with one another to motivate you to continue to create through your purpose. One day you will just know what to do to work with your purpose and accomplish it. At this point your body, spirit and soul have become one in love, light and consciousness, through your soul's purpose in life. Your _essence_ is now one in body, spirit and soul.

All of this is the reality of finding God's purpose for you. God's purpose is not what we should do for God. God's purpose for each and every one of us is to find who we are in body, spirit and soul; then to live our lives through the essential purpose of whom and what we are.

Your quest for your Holy Grail is now complete.

PART 3

THE POWER OF INTENTION IN CREATION

JUDGMENT, DENIAL AND EXPECTATIONS ARE THE POLAR OPPOSITE OF ACCEPTANCE

CREATING YOUR PERSONAL SPIRIT

THIS IS THE TRUE POWER OF INTENTION; THE TRUE POWER OF CREATION

ACCEPTANCE AND ATTRACTION / HARMONY AND BALANCE

CREATING AND MANIFESTING THE SPIRIT OF YOUR REALITY

THE ROLE OF INTENTION IN CREATING YOUR SOUL

CREATING THROUGH RELATIONSHIPS – BONDING WITH OTHERS

CREATING THE SPIRIT OF SMALL GROUPS

SPIRITUAL NOURISHMENT & PERPETUITY

CONSUMPTION – BEING CONSUMED BY THE SPIRIT OF THE REALITY OF YOUR PERSONAL LIFE AND SPIRITUAL EXISTENCE

HOW YOU CREATE YOUR PURPOSE AS IT CONSUMES YOUR LIFE

Creating through love and light

The law of creation is very simple

"WE MUST ALL ALWAYS STRIVE TO CREATE LIGHT.
WE MUST ALL ALWAYS STRIVE TO LOVE COMPLETELY.
WE MUST ALWAYS SHARE THAT LOVE WITH OTHERS BY LIVING WITH LIGHT IN OUR SPIRITS, LOVE IN OUR HEARTS AND CREATING HIGH QUALITY RELATIONSHIPS WITH OTHERS."

ANOTHER WAY OF SAYING THIS IS TO, "LOVE COMEPLTELY AND THEN LOVE YOUR NEIGHBOR AS YOURSELF"

The realities of nature are about the realities associated with our life that occur naturally; they occur through nature. A person's spirit will naturally lose its light and then we work to make it strong again because this is what life is all about. If our spirit was strong enough to exist in the world without being broken it would not need to have a human experience.

The realities of creation are about the processes of creation that exist to help our spirit and soul regain their light and become one again in body, spirit and soul.

The first reality of creation is, "In order to create light you must first live in light".

As a person's spirit evolves through the processes and realities discussed earlier in this book you will learn the power that comes with re-creating your spirit. You can now use your spirit to create a better life for yourself. While making your life better you will make the collective spirit of mankind a little brighter and make the ambient spirit in the world a little brighter also.

In order to make the world a better place a person must have light in their spirit and love in their heart and then share it with others.

When you have a spirit that is capable of holding light and then use it by sharing love and light with everyone you meet, you will naturally create light in the ambient spirit that exists all around the world. It is through every love-based thought, word or action that you have throughout the day that you create more of that which you are at that moment of creation.

The three things needed for spiritual creations to occur are an intention, the emotion that accompanies that intention and the thoughts, words and/or actions that bring them together as the spirit of your intention. The essence of that which you create will be a function of the essence of that which motivates you to act, think or speak at the moment of creation. For example if your intention is to purchase something from the store and the reason you need it is because you are mad at someone, therefore you are binge buying to try to forget that someone hurt your feelings – you are buying through the wants and needs of the essence of greed. This essence will also become a part of that which you create while you are on this shop 'til you drop binge. The spirit of the purchase will exist in the item you buy and stay in it over time. As the things you need to have in your life are a part of your life – it is like having a relationship with these things instead of with people. This is why many people love their dogs or cars more than they do other people. This is what is meant by worshipping idols. It is a natural thing to do when you live with a broken spirit and creating high quality relationships with others is just as natural when your spirit heals.

When you put emotions into something like forgiving you create the spirit of forgiving. In the same manner when Jesus forgave those that hurt him for the sole purpose of forgiving them. His essence created the spirit of forgiveness in the collective spirit of mankind and in the ambient spirit of the world. You create through your personal essence only after you have a spirit that feeds off the love and light of the heavens. When your spirit is not capable of holding light you will be motivated to act by the essence of the spirit or either greed, lust, gluttony, sloth, pride or envy. This is how the essence of these darker spirits perpetuates themselves in our lives. Over time we are eliminating these darker spirits from the collective spirit of mankind.

LIVING WITH JUDGMENT DENIAL AND EXPECTATIONS THAT ARE THE POLAR OPPOSITE OF ACCEPTANCE

When a person lives in an environment that is hurtful it is only natural that he or she will lose their light, love and the ability to forgive those that created the hurtful environment. In a spirit that is not capable of holding light - anger, hatred and rage flourish. As the light in a person's spirit dims through these various levels of darker emotions a person will naturally learn to deny that anger is a bad thing and deny the hurtful things they do to others is wrong. This is common in athletes as their coaches teach them to channel their inner anger in order to be stronger competitors. As this denial continues a person will learn to deny the guidance that comes from light-based spirit that exists in the light side of the heavens. The more someone's personal spirit fills with darkness the harder it is to hear and follow the guidance that comes from the light side of the heavens. When in the darkest state of mind a person will allow himself or herself to be guided by the spirit of others that are in the same dark state of mind. As a person accepts the guidance of those that have a spirit that is also dark it is inevitable that you will deny your-self while accepting this darker guidance. As you deny your-self the essence of who you are becomes hidden in your denial. As a person lives with a darker spirit, it is the spirit of others that are of equal or greater darkness that teaches you how to survive in this state of mind.

This is how the darker side of the collective spirit of mankind works. We all have a spirit that vibrates in a certain way. There are many people with a similar vibration. All those that have a similar vibration are naturally attracted to one another. This collection of spirits that all vibrate together act as one and need one another to maintain their strength in spirit. This is how each of us is effected by the spirit of others that have the same or similar vibration. We receive guidance through the thoughts of others as to how to live in the reality of this spiritual vibration.

BEING JUDGED BY THE JURY OF YOUR FEARS

When you judge others in your life your spirit becomes one with the spirit of all others that have judging spirits. It is like there is a pool of people that all have the same spirit as yourself. The first time you judge someone it is like wading into the shallow end of the pool. You test the waters to see if feels OK to be there; to be in that state of mind. It is like when you first feel fear of someone you might judge them and then the fear will go away. Then as time goes on you will have to choose to continue to judge others or to stop. Most people do not feel very bad after the first time they judge someone and the feeling of judging them did make him or her feel better so they do it again. As fears in your life grow you take that next step into the pool of judgment. As you wade farther into this pool the less aware you will become of the reality that existed when you did not judge others. You lose your connection to love and light as your spirit now goes to sleep while you swim with the spirits of others. This process of wading deeper into the pool continues until you learn to swim with the rest of the peoples' spirits that judge others. Then as you continue to judge others and your spirit becomes immersed in the spirit of this pool of judgment you will feel as if you are being judged. It is only natural that this will happen because your spirit has become one with all the others that are now a part of your collective consciousness. Now, the more you feel judged, the more you will judge others. This is what it is like to be judged by the jury of your fears. This becomes a cycle that will control your life. You will be controlled by this judgment until you have inner strength to overcome the feeling of oneness that now feeds you all the good feelings you are capable of feeling. This is why you need a prodigal son moment to begin the healing process that will free you of this suppressive and oppressive spirit that now consumes you.

This is why it becomes very difficult to just do the right thing when you live with a spirit that is not capable of holding light. In this situation you live with denial and do not accept that you are doing anything wrong. In this state of existence you naturally feel a lot of bad feelings and these feelings go away when you do something hurtful to others. When I have bad feelings they are fear and anger-based feelings that begin by making you feel uncomfortable in certain situations – they may begin as a sort of discomfort in your solar plexus area or in your stomach. If you are having a conversation with someone and you do not agree with what someone else has to say you might get this feeling. If you do not act on this discomfort it will get stronger and you might begin to get upset and anger will begin to build-up in your conversation. As you share a little anger in your conversation you will feel better because your spirit is getting its anger out. As the spirit of your conversation grows into even more anger you will feel even better as you go toe-to-toe with your adversary. As the conversation grows from a discussion to a debate the anger of the spirit of your words and the other person's words continue to grow into a heated argument. If the two people in the argument are not careful hatred will enter the spirit of the argument as the argument grows into a fight. If hatred fills the air in the room the fight will get out of control and this is when two people that were friends end up not talking to each other. When one person feels as if his or her point is the better point and is going to win the argument there is more anger that flows through the spirit of your words of the argument and into the ambient air in the room around them. The other person feels the anger of the spirit of these words and then replies with the same or greater amount of anger through his words. When there is less anger in your spirit you will feel better. When two people use these arguments to express their anger they will naturally feel better after all that anger leaves their spirit – this is when they feel close to the other person. They feel close because, if it was not for the other person they would still feel anger. When a person lives with a great deal of anger and then meets someone that can take that anger away from them they often mistake this lack of anger for love.

This is how anger works. As a person expresses anger they lower the amount of anger in their spirit and this makes them feel better. It is like getting a spiritual reward for being angry. This is why it is so hard to accept that expressing anger is a bad thing. This is how denial enters a person's life. If a person can feel a lot better about himself by expressing anger it becomes natural to deny that there is anything wrong with it.

DENIAL

Denial rules your life when in the darker side of the heavens. Manipulation and deception become the way of life that exists in your mind and in your life. Living with ulterior motives and a reason for everything you do instead of with a sincere intention are some of the characteristics of this reality in life. In this way of life you think before you feel or act; quite often you only think and then act without any feeling for what you are doing. You live with thoughts of denial that manipulate you into believing that your hurtful actions are justified. It becomes a way of life to manipulate other people's opinions of you. When you need to make others think they know who you are is the art of using your words to deceive or to create a belief in others as to who they think you are. Coming up with words that you use to describe who you are in an attempt to frame a person's opinion of you is how a manipulator attempts to use you. Once a person accepts a manipulators words and believes this false perception; the manipulator can now use you (and your spirit) to do the things they need to do so they can perpetuate what they are creating by deceiving you.

The more people that buy into the manipulators stories or lies the stronger his or her network of friends becomes. This network continues to grow and those within the network share the anger, manipulation and deception that are the foundation of a manipulators friendships. Many manipulators are very skilled at deceiving people in such a way as to convince them that they are legitimate; but they are not. This is how called wearing a mask of deception. When a person catches on to the deception and manipulation he or she simply move on to another social group and begin building positive relationships all over again.

Over time this reality just simply becomes a way of life for a manipulator. As you accept yourself as the image that you created in your mind and continue to deny the reality that exists around you. All your thoughts are designed around what to say to people and how to create this image that you want to project. A big part of the image you try to create is an image as if you have never done anything wrong or hurtful to anyone. It is easy for a manipulator to say that they made a mistake but will always say it with no feeling or remorse while talking about someone else who is more wrong than they are. In a way they are just saying that they are wrong but others are more wrong and in this way justifying their actions. If someone tries to point out that they are not as perfect as they try to present themselves they will feel the anger, hatred and rage they strive to contain through the image they create. They will also justify directing your anger towards this person as if, "Who does she think she is to say that about me". Eventually they will get to a point in their life where the deceptions and manipulations can no longer be maintained and their world crumbles around you. At this point they will either become more deceptive and manipulative as their spirit becomes even darker or will learn to change.

This change begins with accepting the truths about who you are and the hurtful things you did to others and to yourself. By accepting yourself for the good, the bad and the ugly that you are and the things you have done in your life you are overcoming the need to be perfect. Face it you are not alone – we have all done things we are not proud of. This is a reality in our lives and accepting that we are not perfect is one of the most powerful healing realities we can create for ourselves. This is the biggest step in the process of accepting yourself. As you accept yourself, the denial that trapped you into this darker state of mind will no longer control your life.

Acceptance is a critical aspect of your spirit that you will just naturally grow when the time is right.

CREATING YOUR PERSONAL SPIRIT

When a person has an intention to do the right thing for someone, his or her spirit fills with the light that is a reflection of that intention. The light then flows from your spirit and out of you through every thought, word or action. This is a state of nature. It is only natural for you to create your own personal spirit and then to create the spirit of your thoughts words and actions as well to create the spirit of your relationships. It is that easy and it is that complicated. Easy because it sounds like you just have to wish it or want it and it will somehow magically happen. It is not that simple. In order to create light your intention has to be sincere. You cannot just think that you are doing something for the right reason and then also have an intention or ulterior motive for what you are doing. It is not like multi-tasking where you can do several things at once in order to accomplish an objective; you cannot have multiple intentions and expect to create through the one that you want to create through; it just does not work that way. If you want to do the right thing but what truly motivates your thoughts, words and actions is something else, then this other motivator – this ulterior motive is what your spirit will create through.

> If you want to do something to help someone and you need to make money for the work you do; so you do a good deed but then charge someone a lot of money for what you did for them; which of these two intentions do you think you will create through?

> You will create through the lesser intention that motivate you to act – the need to make money.

That which you are truly committed too is that through which you will create and it is what you will create in your own personal spirit. If you are trying to make a change in your life and struggle to make it better – look closely at what you are doing and what truly motivates your actions. If you change this – over time you will realize that you are no longer afraid of losing money or not having what you need and the reality in your life will change. This does not mean that you need to give all your money away in order to change your reality. It means that you need to understand what your motivators are and try to change them. This will allow you to be more true to your intention instead of denying your true intention because you want to convince yourself that you are doing something for another reason. If you want people to think you care about them so you ask them a question and then wait to make a comment so you can then tell them about your life – are you more committed to hear about the other person or about talking about yourself. I am using this as an example because so many of us do this – it is only natural that we do things like this. We need to embrace who we are before you can truly make the changes we strive for. Then you can practice doing what you need to do like actively listening to what others have to say and not comment on what they way instead just accept what he or she has to say or practice being generous for others just for the sake of being generous. As I wrote these books I truly want to share what I learned about how the spirit of mankind works. The information was given to me because I truly wanted to know the truth. I was sincere and now I only want to share what I learned with you.

If you love a little you will be forgiven a little if you love a lot you will be forgiven a lot. If you are sincere you will receive sincerity in your spirit if you are insincere you will receive insincerity in your spirit. If you accept others for who they are you will create acceptance in your spirit; then feel accepted by others. If you have a lot of expectations you will eventually become consumed by them and not feel accepted or loved.

You honor your spirit through your intention therefore your intention must be sincere and true to your-self. This does not mean that you have to always be completely righteous in order to create. Just accept that your intention is what it is – be true to it. If you are a car salesman and you need to sell a car in order to make a house payment then be true to your needs. Do not try to convince yourself that every car you try to sell is going to be the perfect car for the person that buys it. You can also be true to your-self by recognizing those people that truly need a good deal and then do your best to make that happen for them. When you are going to help someone get a great deal be true to that intention and go as far as you possibly can to get them that great deal they need.

The impact of this intention on your life is that you will create your spirit to be a reflection of who you are. Your intention will then generate through the essence of the spirit that is you. You will then feel the light or dark of your intentions. This is how powerful your intention is. It creates your spirit and then controls your soul. The more positive your intentions the greater the vibration your spirit will be and then it will attract to you people that are of the same vibration. If you are only interested in selling a car and you believe that you are the best negotiator – you will attract others that are of like spirit. This means that others that enjoy engaging in a negotiation that centers on giving the least and getting the most will be attracted to you and then you can both engage in a negotiation that will make you both feel good. This does not mean that everyone that crosses your path will be someone that is a negotiator – it just simply means that those that are negotiators will recognize your spirit and then engage in negotiations with you accordingly and you will both enjoy the interaction. Two people with similar non-emotional spiritual characteristics will create a spirit that has no love in it but they will feel good about themselves as both parties will walk away feeling as if they got the most out of their side of the deal.

If, on the other hand, you were to dedicate your intentions to always finding the right car for the right person to meet their budgetary needs – to meet or exceed their expectations – you will create a spirit that will attract more people that just want to buy a good car, to you. They will sense and feel your spirit even as they are driving past your dealership. This kind of attraction just happens naturally as your intention creates the spirit of your business. It takes time to transform a spirit that wants to just sell a car to someone into a spirit that will attract more people to you so you can help them. But, when it is done you will feel better about your job, generate more return customers and get more referrals from those customers that are satisfied with the cars they purchase from you. You have to walk the talk not just talk the talk.

THIS IS THE TRUE POWER OF INTENTION; THE TRUE POWER OF CREATION

IN ORDER TO CREATE LIGHT YOU MUST FIRST LIVE IN LIGHT

FIRST YOU HAVE TO CREATE FORGIVENESS IN YOUR SPIRIT – CREATE A FORGIVING SPIRIT

When a person loses his or her love it is not long until the capability to forgive others is lost. Without forgiveness in your spirit and life, your spirit cannot hold light. The natural feeling of love in your life is lost until you re-create forgiveness in your spirit. Forgiveness will then bring some light into your spirit and love into your heart. As you continue the process of creating forgiveness in your spirit you will grow a spirit capable of holding more light and then feel a greater love in your heart. Forgiveness is the fundamental vibration in your spirit. It is the foundation on which love is built. All the aspects of you, your spirit and your personality are built from a foundation in love, light and forgiveness. Without forgiveness there is no light, no love and therefore no ability to create other aspects of you into your life. Other aspects of you might be acceptance of others, being nonjudgmental, grace, peace of mind, wisdom or being merciful. All these aspects of you come from your spirit and they can only exist if you have light in your spirit and love in your heart. It is the strength of your spirit and soul that will allow these characteristics to flourish within you. Just like the process of creation will create forgiveness in your spirit; through an intention to forgive combined with love creates through your thoughts, words and actions. Other aspects of who you are can be created in the same manner. Without love and light there is no power to create these positive aspects of you in or through your spirit.

ACCEPTANCE AND ATTRACTION / HARMONY AND BALANCE

ACCEPTANCE

ACCEPTANCE IMPROVES THE QUALITY OF YOUR SPIRIT AND THE BLOOD OF LIFE THAT FILLS YOUR CUPS

Acceptance is an interesting reality and process of creation. Acceptance begins with accepting your personal spirit and the light it is capable of holding. In this way you accept you, your-self.

You accept the first level transformation into your life by allowing your spirit to fill with light. Then, when you allow yourself to feel the love that accompanies this light you are beginning to accept your spirit. As you continue to allow yourself to feel the love that comes from your spirit it is only natural that you will be motivated to act on these love-based-feelings. As you share your love and light with others you are learning to co-create with others as you create love-based relationships.

The second level of acceptance is to allow your souls consciousness to guide you into the light. It is with thoughts and feelings that you will develop a harmony within your body, spirit and soul. Harmony will allow you to grow from one level of acceptance to another and to maintain your love and light along the way. As your soul grows through the love of your spirit; you will learn to accept and trust theses more peaceful thoughts that enter your consciousness. This second level of acceptance of feelings and thoughts will continue to develop as your relationships with others continues to grow. As you learn to accept others into your life you will naturally be more honest about who you are. Since you are being attracted to others that are more accepting you will not feel judged by them nor will you feel like judging them.

As relationships in your life change you are experiencing the third level of acceptance. As you accept others into your life and in some cases you will reject those that used to be in your life. When your spirit was not capable of holding light you attracted a different kind of person into your life. By creating acceptance in your spirit you will find it much easier to just get along with people. The conflict and judgment that existed in previous relationships will fade away. This is when you might realize that you are more capable of just accepting others for who they are without any expectations of them. While you will be more accepting of others you will also sense and feel things about those that were friends before your spirit changed. When this happens you will sense and feel differently about them because you will feel the negativity of their intentions (their ulterior motives to use you). This will make you feel uncomfortable about being around them and motivate you to spend more time with others that are of like spirit to your-self.

The fourth level of acceptance is when you learn to accept your spiritual gifts. Your ability to sense and feel the spirit of others is the first step into your spiritual gifts. This is when you become sensitive to others and their spirit. At this level of sensitivity you will also become sensitive to the intentions of others as you feel either the hurtful nature of their thoughts, words and actions or the sincerity of their intentions towards you. Learning to accept them even though they are trying to intentionally hurt you will allow your spirit to grow to have an even stronger connection to your soul. This is what loving your enemy is all about. Learning to love others even if you sense they do not have your best interest at heart. As your spirit becomes bright, spiritual gifts become part of your life. As you learn to sense the spirit around you and become more empathic it is natural to grow a healer's heart. It is the sensitivity that comes with being empathic that will naturally motivate a person to want to help others. The desire to help others can bring healing gifts into a person's life.

As you accept others at an even higher level your spirit and soul develop into the fifth level of acceptance. With this level of understanding or conscious awareness as to who they are, you will see others in a new light. In this light you can easily understand why some people do hurtful things to others. At this level you can sense the spirit of the man or woman, not just hear their words but truly sense who they are. As you develop the skill to sense and feel you may even understand why they are the kind of person they are; why they might be so self-centered. This will allow you to just know the person at such a deep level that your sympathy and empathy takes over as you feel their pain. At this point in your overall spiritual development you will forgive them for they know not what they do. When you have carried your cross and become one integrated in body, spirit and soul you have grown as a person and in spirit. This is the result of the issues in your life. After your essence has resurrected through your spirit and soul's human experience you will naturally grow into this heightened level of awareness.

ATTRACTION

Attraction is a reality of the vibration of your spirit. As your spirit vibrates without the capability of holding light you will be attracted to associate with others that have the same limited capability to hold light. When you live with fear and anger forces at work within your body spirit and soul repel your body, spirit and soul. Love attracts and anger repels.

As your spirit grows into a rhythm and vibration that is light-based you will naturally be attracted to those that have the same basic spirit.

As you live with a life filled with purpose the essence of your purpose will feed you what you need in order to fulfill your purpose. Celebrities that live with a purpose to make the world a better place attract to them what they need in order to feed their purpose. This includes what they need in order to feed and clothe them in the physical as well as feed their purpose in a spiritual way.

HARMONY & BALANCE

The reason this book explains all the realities that exist in both dark and light states of mind is to share with you the idea that all is good; that all are acceptable states of mind and ways of life. An individual person has to find his or her own peace and peace of mind at his or her own pace. Harmony exists when a person feels comfortable in his or her own existence with the thoughts and feelings they live with. Change will bring disharmony to the state of peace that existed in a person's mind and way of life. This is when a new reality will grow from the lack of harmony and balance that change will naturally create. Helping you manage these moments of change is what this book is all about.

In a less than light state of mind, harmony exists when everything is in the right place – whether it is things in a house or work place. Relationships can also be viewed as important to having harmony in your life. When something changes or if the pieces do not fit the way you need them to fit disharmony will exist in your spirit and you will feel anxious, upset or even angry. This is disharmony. In this less than light spiritual realty it is normal to strive to make everything fit the way you need them to fit so your anxiety will go away. This leads to having expectation of others and of things as if everything must go the way you want and need them to go or something bad will happen or a negative thought about yourself will enter your mind.

GREED VS. GENEROSITY (THE THIRD HORSEMAN OF REVELATIONS)

In a light state of mind harmony exists in many different ways. There is no longer a need to control things and people to try to make them be the way you want them to be. With light in your spirit and peace in your heart you will feel more comfortable just going with the flow of life. As people come and go throughout your life you will not feel a sense of harmony and disharmony instead you will just feel grateful that you had those moments with them.

In Revelations there is an image that is referred to as the third horseman. It is seen as a rider on a horse that is carrying a scale and there are people in the background talking about how they have to buy merchandise and how they want to make sure it is of the best possible quality for their money. This image is about the reality in creation that everything is an exchange. We create the spirit of the exchange as well as the actual exchange in the physical. When a person tries to buy something and all his or her attention is centered on the best deal for himself or herself; this person is not capable of being grateful for the opportunity to be there in that moment. It is a much colder reality and it prevents and blocks our spirit from feeling grateful. Try it sometime go out to buy something and when it costs more than you want to pay for it -– Are you really grateful for what you are buying or does the price make it less enjoyable?

BALANCE – GIVING AND RECEIVING

When living with a darker spirit, balance is about taking and paying; it is about giving very little and taking as much as you can while doing very little for it.

When people begin to develop a less dark or lighter spirit they will naturally be drawn to make exchanges that are more about giving and receiving. There is a difference between taking and receiving. To receive is to allow someone to give you something instead the feeling of a need to take what you can get. This opens your spirit to feeling grateful and being generous. Being grateful and generous go hand in hand - as you become more generous you will feel more grateful for the things you have in life. As people no longer need things in their life to make them feel good it is only natural that we will learn to be more generous and grateful. This is how we evolve into a better way of life.

When people are truly in a light state of mind they will share. To share means to give and to receive equally. Many people that have not grown into a true light spirit tend to over-give, in a sense, as they feel like it is better to give than to receive. To just do for others and to not allow others to do for you is not going to create balance in your life. It is important to have balance in your life by doing both giving and receiving.

When a person lives in such a way as to over react to situations he or she will create a spirit that will feed off of the nature of over reacting. This creates a spirit that will need to be consumed by this type of behavior in order to feel like it is in balance. When a spirit is very weak (slothful) it will need to be consumed by the need to do something in order to react. People that are severely depressed do not have a sense of urgency to act; people that are even more consumed by depression have no sense of emergency. This is why some people can hear a baby crying or drive past an accident and not react to it at all.

A spirit that exists through wants and needs, desires and cravings will exist with a different sense of harmony and balance than a spirit that holds light and thrives on having a life filled with purpose. When a person lives with the cravings of wants, needs and desires he or she will strive to have everything in its place; relationships and things need to be in order or the anger, fear, resentment or other feelings they are trying to suppress will manifest in their lives. This leads to having expectations of others. When others do what you need or expect them to do these fears and anger can be suppressed. As this type of person feeds off the need to have more expectations of others a cycle that consumes her or his spirit will evolve. Eventually these expectations will lead to relationships that need to have more expectations and then even more until no one can achieve the expectations. This is when relationships begin to falter. It is just like parents that try to control their children through rules. Once these rules become so over-powering (consuming) to the children, the children act out just so they can feel like they can breathe. Parents become consumed by creating rules and expectations and then the children become consumed by the suppressive nature of them. This is how parents can feel good about themselves as parents while simultaneously create a hurtful environment for their family and never realize they are doing it.

We are not talking about rules that create a safe environment for a child to live in. We are talking about becoming consumed by making rules.

If a person stops the behaviors that make them feel good by suppressing anger, the thoughts and feelings that motivated them to do it in the first place will become stronger. Without the behaviors that suppressed the anger you might be motivated you to create more expectations. It will be as if feelings and thoughts in your heart and mind might tell you that you are not a good parent or that you are a loser or in some other way are no good. These thoughts and feelings might go away when you make a rule but the underlying issues that created those thoughts and feelings still exist. It is these underlying truths that you suppress that are the root cause of your need to set expectations. Stopping these behaviors will create an environment that will force a person to deal with her or his issues in life and the quest to create a grail cup will begin.

Balance exists in this person's life when everything is where it belongs, and everyone says and does as they are told or manipulated to do. There is a sort of harmony that comes with the rhythm of expecting everything to be done in a certain way as if as long as everything works the way it should and everyone says and does what they should, you will not feel anger or disappointment and life is good. The reality of this way of life is that fear and anger will always strive to exist in your life. As fear and anger bubble up through all the things and people that eventually cannot do what you need them to do, disharmony will exist. This type of disharmony will lead to a spirit that will either grow darker or you will pick up your cross and walk your path to learn how to eliminate anger and create a healthy balance in your life.

Balance and harmony exist in different ways when in light or in dark states of mind. A healthy balance and harmony exist when we no longer have expectations and just accept the chaos in life as just the way life is. Therefore what many people think of as harmony may not exist as a permanent reality in our lives.

When we are at peace with the issues in our lives, when we live with unconditional love in our hearts and share that love throughout our lives we have achieved a state of mind that is at peace; balance and harmony will exist in our spirit even though there may be disharmony in the world around us. It is a state of mind that does not rely on others or any-thing to maintain it. You merely have to accept others for who they are and have no expectations.

MANIFESTING THE SPIRIT OF YOUR REALITY

The ambient spirit is the spirit that we manifest in the air around us. It is a function of our overall intention's and our spirit's capability to process light. You are capable of processing a certain amount of light throughout your day to day interactions. The amount of light you are capable of processing is a function of the love in your life, how committed you are to sharing it with others and the intensity of your commitment to your purpose in life (in light) or determination to survive (in dark).

A person with a spirit that is only capable of processing a little bit of light is capable of processing no more than a little bit of light. A person whose spirit is sealed away from light is not capable of processing any light at all. The reality you can manifest in your life is a function of the light you process through your spirit. This is why "if you want to create (manifest) light you must first live in light".

The ambient spirit is also a function of the collective spirit of mankind. How we interact with others is what will manifest the ambient spirit that is in the air all around the world. Since we collectively have a certain amount of light and dark in all of us collectively it is only natural that the ambient spirit in the air will only be as light or dark as we are. As two people interact in a lunch room they will manifest the spirit of the words they speak as they talk about their family life or other coworkers. We do not have to directly interact with someone by talking to them, we can also exchange thoughts with others as we drive to work in the morning. When we are driving to work in the morning and we are late and stressed out we will transfer that stress and anger (road rage) into the ambient air along the interstate. If you find you are in front of a person with road rage and he is driving to close to your car, you do not have to volley his rage back at him. As you try to encourage him to back off all you have to do is send a positive thought to him asking him to give you a little room. Most people are not aware of their impact on others and do not even realize they are driving that close. A simple thought is all it takes to remind him that he is driving that close and most people will back away from your car.

Your intention will determine the amount and quality of light that will flow through you hour-by-hour and from day-to-day. The emotions you are capable of processing will determine the quality and quantity of the spirit you are capable of creating. If you deal with your issues in life and constantly push your-self to have a better intention you will create a spirit that is capable of processing at a higher level; then you will be motivated to do what is necessary to create your spirit so it can hold more light. This is not an easy thing to accomplish. It is especially challenging for teenagers whose hormones are constantly motivating them to act on their feelings and their spirit may not be capable of holding that much light. They can easily become consumed by the spirit of their intentions and then become overwhelmed by them.

When a large quantity of people drive to work and everyone senses and feels the spirit of road rage it is only natural that we will then believe that our rage is justified. It just feels right. This is how the collective spirit impacts each of us in our day to day lives. This is the challenge we all face – to feel the fear and anger; then find a better way. When you can overcome the thoughts and feelings that you live with all day long every day you can create a new reality for your-self. When you overcome the ambient spirit that mankind has created in the communities in which you live you can create an even better reality for your-self.

THE ROLE OF INTENTION IN CREATING YOUR SPIRIT AND SOUL

When you have an intention to do something your spirit fills with the emotion related to the intention (positive or negative). It is like your spirit becomes filled with both the emotion and the intention. As your spirit and soul are filled with this intention and emotion you will receive the thoughts that will guide you to act on your intention and emotion. When you have an intention to say or do something and it is hurtful in nature your spirit will fill with the quality of the emotion of your intention. As you continue to have the same intention throughout your day and then the next day and then the next day you will create the spirit of that hurtful intention in you; in your personal spirit. This becomes your nature; your human nature.

Many people today say that it is only natural to do hurtful things because it is human nature to do so; while others will question how people can do such hurtful things to others. People that have not yet learned to live with love will assume that no can get there; while those that have learned to live with love cannot understand how people can do hurtful things to others. As people are learning to live with love they will not allow themselves to hurt others and will not accept it in others. When human nature reaches an even higher level of light people will be able to accept the good and evil that exists in the world without judgment.

When you lower the vibration of your spirit you will naturally fill it with anger, hatred and rage. Anger, hatred and rage feed greed, lust and gluttony. As a person's intention feeds his or her spirit with anger, hatred and rage it is only natural to create a spirit that will be motivated by greed, lust and gluttony. The essences of the spirit of greed, lust and gluttony are wants and needs, desires and cravings. When the essences of these darker states of mind become a part of your personal spirit they will rule your life until you can overcome them and change the reality of your existence.

If you live with negative intentions you will become filled with needs, desires and cravings throughout your day. It is a state of nature that this reality will exist. To be motivated by the essences of these darker states of mind is to create more of that which you are when your intentions and emotions create through your thoughts words and actions. So when you are motivated by greed or lust and then you act on the thoughts that come with that state of mind you will solidify your spirit and souls presence in that state of mind. This is how you build a home for your spirit and soul and how the reality of lust or greed becomes a part of your life.

When you create through an intention that is always positive you are creating a spirit that is caring, compassionate, generous and grateful. When you feel a sense of being generous and grateful you have created a spirit that does not want or need for any-thing or any-one. When you just feel good about what you say think or do and you openly share your-self with others you are creating a home for your spirit in the light side of the heavens. While accepting others for who they are and feeling grateful just for the chance to share you will find peace and joy in your heart. As we just accept others for who they are and share the essence of who we are with others we will create peace and joy in the ambient spirit of the world.

The best part of creating this in your spirit is that others will feel it too. Whenever you enter a room you will not have to say a word but others will know you are there because they will feel the essence of your spirit.

CREATING THROUGH RELATIONSHIPS – BONDING WITH OTHERS

When creating through an interaction with another person, a bond exists. This interaction creates a spiritual bond between those involved. The strength of the bond is a function of the shared (or common) intention, depth of emotion and time committed to the event that brings their spirits together.

In order for the spirit of two people to create a bond they have to share a common intention and/or a common emotion as they talk to each other or do something together. When the rhythm and vibration of two peoples' intentions and emotions are the same they will create a strong bond. When two people share a motivation that comes from the same state of mind (being generous and grateful, greed or lust), they feel as if they are kindred spirits and will create a strong spiritual bond.

When two people have very different points of views but both are passionately committed to their point of view it is easy to create a bond of respect between them. It is not about what they say or that they agree or disagree; it is about the passion or emotion that they exchange. When two people meet and try to change the other person's point of view; they share an intention and this strengthens the bond between them-selves. This is not always the healthiest bond but it is a weak bond nonetheless. This is a bond of disrespect and can lead to a failed friendship. If the friends volley their differences enough the bond will eventually break.

When a person has a lot of anger and tries to create a bond with another person, but the other person responds with love; a spiritual bond will not be created. As these people share equal and opposite emotions with an intention to create the polar opposite rhythm and vibration as the other person – no bond is created. In this way the best defense is a strong offense. In many cases, as you respond with love, the person generating the anger will continue to try to create and force more of the anger he harbors within him, into your spirit. It is very important that you become very grounded in love as you continue to direct positive thoughts to him.

The strength of this bond between two people is also a function of the actions they share during the moment of creation. When two people talk together and find a common ground on which to agree and find they like each other, an emotional bond is created. When they find they have a common purpose in life a bond of intention is created. When they work together to help each other achieve a goal or purpose they have created a spiritual bond that is filled with purpose.

Children merely have to meet on the street, say. "Hi, my name is Ralph", when the other child replies, "Hi, my name is Sue", they begin to create a spiritual bond. This is because they have such pure spirits that all they want to do is bond with others and share who they are with others and then feed off of the love of their friendships.

CREATING THE SPIRIT OF SMALL GROUPS

The spirits' of two people come together when they agree or share an opinion about something or someone.

For example:

> When two people are talking about someone they truly care about they create the spirit of caring through their conversation. The stronger they care about this person the stronger the feeling of the spirit that exists in the room. When the person they are talking about enters that room he or she will feel cared for because that is the spirit that was created. The two people creating the spirit of caring do not feel the change in the room because their spirits are filled with this feeling of caring. This is how we manifest the ambient spirit of a room. When someone else enters this room it will be filled with this higher vibration and she or he will feel cared for. When the specific person they were talking about enters the room the spirit in the room will be amplified because the person will feel cared for (feed off of the spirit that was created) and then in return generate a caring feeling that will go back into the spirit of the room. Feeding off of this manifested spirit in a room and then feeding it with your own spirit is called spiritual nourishment.

When we become filled with intention and purpose every thought word and action is focused on accomplishing that purpose. It takes a strong spirit and body to be able to process that much love and light. To be constantly creating is an incredible feeling. To feel this power of creation, flowing through you with every thought, word or action creates a sense of feeding off of your purpose. What you accomplish through your day to day focus on your goals and objectives is creation at its best. When a person is working at his or her job and truly loves the work he or she is doing there is an incredible feeling of satisfaction that comes from it (from the spirit of their creation). Just like when a person truly loves raising children; at the end of the day you may be exhausted but nonetheless you have a feeling of satisfaction. As a person's spirit becomes strong enough to live with purpose the next step is to make it strong enough to work with others. The more we love others and our purpose the brighter our spirit will flow (glow). As you work as a team you create the spirit of the team; the marines call this esprit de corps – the spirit of the marine corp.

When a classroom has a teacher with a passion to teach and is filled with students that all want to learn; the room is filled with the spirit of learning. But, it only takes one or two students that are not able to maintain an intense focus and commitment to learning, to shift the spirit in the room. When the spirit in the room is not completely focused on learning and teaching this weaker spirit will impact others, even those with a desire to learn and it can impact the teacher lowering his or her desire to teach. When the students (or just some of the students) are not capable of processing enough light through their spirit to stay focused all day long, the spirit in the room will be affected by them and in a big way. This lower vibrating spirit will impact others that might be struggling to pay attention. It is very common for a student, trying to pay attention, to have his or her spirit impacted by another student's spirit. The anger-based thoughts and intentions of one student can encourage another student to act out in the classroom. A classroom of teenagers is the most demanding collection of uncontrolled spirits that exist today. It is a challenge for the individual student, it is a challenge for the classroom of students and it is a challenge for the teacher.

I hope you can see why it is very difficult if not impossible to create the spirit of learning in a classroom with more than 10 teenagers. It is more that we can expect that they stay focused on learning all the various subjects for 8 hours a day, five days a week, for nine to ten months per year.

Very few teachers and very few students have a spirit that is capable of maintaining such a high level of focus on their subject matter all day long. It is not always the case that a student does not want to stay focused it is just that their spirit is not capable of processing that much light for such a long period of time. It takes a very healthy spirit to maintain a strong sense of purpose for such long periods of time.

This is why some schools that teach the students what they want to learn are so successful. When you teach people what they want to learn they will have more fun learning; this creates a healthier more focused spirit between the student and the teacher. This is how to create a learning environment how to create the spirit of learning. This environment creates faith between the teacher and the student. The spirit of faith is a very powerful reality of success.

SPIRITUAL NOURISHMENT & PERPETUITY

SPIRITUAL NOURISHMENT

That which you create will feed its-self and feed you.

It will feed you the same feelings and intentions that you felt at the moment of its creation.

It will strive to feed off of you by motivating you to re-create the emotions and intentions that existed at the moment of its creation. It is like creating a child in your spirit.

When you receive a feeling and thoughts from the past and then express them you feed these spiritual children that you created.

This is one of the most interactive realities of creation. You can be consumed by that which you create. Some people need to be consumed by an event before they will feel anything at all. When someone is depressed he or she will need to be faced with an overwhelming amount of reality before reacting to it while a person that has a healthier spirit will be consumed by his or her purpose in life.

When people enter the spirit of someone that is depressed they might feel emotionally or energetically drained. This is because there is no rhythm or vibration in the spirit of depression. With no life in their spirit there is no life in the home of this person either. With no life in a person's spirit there is no motivation to live, no reason to get up in the morning. You can help a person put life back into his or her spirit. One of the best ways is to encourage them to find the memories that made them feel very sad or very fearful. Then to encourage them to let go of the feelings they have been holding inside; encourage them to cry if that is what they feel like doing. When they release these emotions that they have been suppressing for so long it will tend to cleanse their spirit. This will make room for other emotions to enter as they begin to create rhythm in their spirit again.

PERPETUITY

That which you create in spirit will want to perpetuate its existence; it wants to live.

In your personal spirit, all your intentions will strive to live. They want to survive and they will feed off you and your emotions until you either transform them or allow them to fade away and die. The depth of the intentions and emotions that are experienced when these spiritual children are born (or created) will determine its strength and will to survive. The depth of emotions and intentions will also determine how great their impact will be on you as they strive to feed off your emotions.

You allow these creations to exist in your spirit (in your mind) by feeding them.

You allow them to change by feeding them a different intention, thought or emotion.

When they change they will now strive to feed off the new intentions and feelings that they exist with.

PLEASE REMEMBER:

The hurtful intentions behind your actions create a bond in your spirit with those that you hurt. This bond will rule your life as you live with the spirit of your intentions and the essence of that which you create.

The positive loving intentions behind your actions create a bond with those that will feed you the love and light that will nourish your spirit and soul. This spiritual bond will exist through both people involved with this co-creation. It will continue to grow and create a spirit that will guide you into a better way of life.

Forgiveness will transform the spiritual bond that was created in a child that was hurt by a parent, sibling or others. Forgiveness changes the polarity of the spiritual bond that was created when a person experiences suffering. When a person can no longer forgive the hurtful things others do and reaches into the pit of their stomach and says I will never forgive him or her or says they hate another person they reverse the polarity of their personal spirit. This is how we create a seal that seals our spirit into a darker reality. Later in life when we try to forgive that person we have to forgive with the same strength that we felt when we were able to forgive and love with the same strength in hatred that created the seal that sealed our fate.

CONSUMPTION – BEING CONSUMED BY THE SPIRIT OF THE REALITY OF YOUR PERSONAL LIFE AND SPIRITUAL EXISTENCE

In general terms there are two ways to view this reality:

1) To be consumed by the spirit and way of life that exists when a child or generation of children are born into the world and are:
    a. Consumed by the way of life that exists in the world
    b. Consumed by the issues from their past life (lives)
2) To be consumed by the reality you create for your-self through your thoughts, words and actions – This can be the consumption that exists when a person lives an obsessive compulsive way of life or when a person is consumed by his or her purpose in life.

THE LIGHT OF A CHILD'S SPIRIT WHEN IT IS CONSUMED BY THE SPIRIT OF THE WORLD THEY ENTER

A person ends a past-life with a limited amount of light in his or her spirit and issues that have not yet been dealt with. The effect of these issues still limits the light that could exist in a person's spirit in a future life-time. When a child enters the world it is only natural that he or she will come into the world with more love and light than he or she left the world with in his or her past life. Between the time of ca person's part life and current life the spirit of the world changes; it evolves and grows lighter. When a child enters this better collective spirit it receives a spiritual boost as it enters. This spiritual boost will bring its spirit up to a level that will help it deal with the issues from its past life early on in its life.

Throughout a life-time children will lose this light as life's realities create an environment that makes it difficult to maintain it. This is how they begin to become consumed by the spirit of the collective spirit of mankind. Coming into the world with a greater love and light sets a standard or level of light in your spirit that will motivate you to strive to achieve the changes you need to overcome throughout your lifetime.

The spirit of a generation of children enter the world with a collective purpose. That purpose is for a generation of children to shift the amount of light that exists in the collective spirit in a positive direction. This purpose comes from the prayers and desires of people that want to make the world a better place. As people have deep seeded desires they reach into the pit of their stomach and create the spirit of their desire. This deep seeded desire feeds the purpose of future generations. When people pray with the same feelings that come from the pit of their stomach they create the spirit of their prayer. This is matures way; it is creations way of making the world a better place.

One way to imagine this is as if the spirit of children entering the world comes through the stratosphere that surround the earth. The stratosphere contains the collective spirit of the world. The stratosphere is lighter or brighter that it was when the spirit of a child left the world in its past life and contains the prayers and desires of those that live in the world at that point in time. This gives the spirit of children entering the world a boost and their purpose in life. This creates the spirit of children that are consumed by the collective spirit of mankind at that moment in time.

Children come into the world as part of a generation of children with a purpose and light that is unique to them. It takes lifetime to accomplish these changes. Throughout this life time they will bring a greater light into the world and love their light as they become consumed by the reality of life and the hardships that come with living in a world with a full range of light and dark that still exists in it.

As time goes on they will continue to be bundles of love that bring joy into the hearts of others. Then one day they will have an experience that will bring fear into their life. If they do not act on the fear in an appropriate way (avoid the situation the fear is warning them about) they will experience sadness. As fear and sadness grow in their spirit they will most likely learn to live with fear and sadness. As fear grows in a person's spirit it he or she will become afraid; this is the first indication that fear is becoming unhealthy. As their spirit becomes consumed with these two feelings (fear and sadness) they will learn to ignore or deny them. For many centuries boys were raised to feel the fear and do it anyways or to just ignore fear and suppress sadness. Sometimes denying fear and sadness is the only way to deal with life when the environment you live in is filled with situations that cause fear and sadness. To be afraid is to live with fear – this is the first step into a darker reality in your life. Fear and being consumed by fear leads to living with anger.

As time goes on in this person's life he or she will begin to deal with the issues that evolved from an unhealthy environment; then he or she will feel the fear and learn what it is trying to tell you. As your spirit becomes healthier the weaker states of their mind will no longer prevent you from feeling sad and you will learn to express all your feelings whether they are joyful, sadness or fear.

As your spirit heals, fear will become a healthy ally that warns you of impending dangers; sadness will become a feeling that you live to allow yourself to express. Expressing sadness is an important part of changing the rhythm and vibration of an unhealthy spirit into the rhythm and vibration that is more natural to the essence of your personal spirit.

The healing process is about integrating various parts of your spirit into one whole healthy spirit. There is a big difference between a man becoming aware of his feminine side and integrating it into his spirit completely. Living a whole and healthy way of life is what living a holistic lifestyle is all about – becoming one in body, spirit and soul. Integrating these various aspects (inner child, masculine or feminine aspects) of you into your spirit will make your spirit stronger. This will make you healthier emotionally and your spirit more balanced as a result of this integration. A person's spirit will grow mature with this higher light and love as he or she learns to re-create their spirit. A healthier spirit will be able to hold this brighter light and live to accomplish a greater purpose. At the same time the current life-style and the spirit that was created by previous generations will work against them, when they are very young. All these forces of nature and creation are constantly at work within the minds of children. Children have all this love to share as they become consumed by the life-style and spirit of the world around them. At a young age, when children have this greater light in their spirit, they will be able to more effectively deal with the issues from their past life. Most children deal with many issues from their past lives before they are 8 years old.

After they learn to control their thoughts, words and actions they will re-create their spirit and learn to live with love and light again. When this happens your spirit is maturing and preparing itself to handle an even brighter light. This brighter light is the light of your purpose.

HOW YOU CREATE YOUR PURPOSE AS IT CONSUMES YOUR LIFE

BEING COMSUMED BY LIGHT

As your life fills with purpose you will naturally continue to strengthen your spirit as you become consumed by the spirit of your purpose in life. When consumed by all the things that make you feel good or great about your life it is easy to focus on just one or two things that you feel compelled to do. While it is good or even great to have this purpose filled life it is also important to remember that you need balance and to not become over consumed by any one aspect of who you are and what your spirit is becoming. As you find that something that is your spirits purpose you will grow into a balanced life that will be consumed by your spirit and your individual purpose. Your individual purpose will be linked to your generation's purpose and then your spirits purpose will grow beyond your generation's purpose.

As your personal spirit and soul aligns with the spirit and purpose of your generation your essence will grow into your life through your purpose.

As your spirit shines bright it is processing more light through it. As your purposeful life grows from your individual purpose into your generation's purpose your spirit will shine even brighter. When you live to allow your spirit's purpose to be the most important part of your life your spirit will shine its brightest. When you spirit overflows with the passion of your life's purpose your spirit is like a cup that is getting larger as the needs of your purpose increase. As the needs of your purpose increase your spirit gets larger, the amount of light it processes increases and your cup over flows and glows.

BEING CONSUMED WHEN YOUR SPIRIT CANNOT HOLD LIGHT

Some people have to overindulge in something in order to feel anything at all while others need to over-emote in order to try to convince themselves and others they live with a love-based spirit. When a person becomes obsessive about loving others as if you have to always pull yourself from one lower emotion like sadness to another extreme like loving others or caring for someone you are over-emoting. Over-emoting has three faces it can be:

1) an attempt to force your-self to feel
2) an attempt to force yourself to feel good
3) an attempt to convince others that you are in a positive loving state of emotion

These are normal states of mind and realities for many if not most people today.

When trying to convince others that you are in a positive loving state of emotion you are wearing a mask of deception. People often deceive themselves while trying to convince themselves that they do not have a problem. One of the most challenging states of mind to be in is denial.

Some people are sympathetic to other people's feelings; while others try to use sympathy to get attention. Using sympathy to get someone else's attention is a form of manipulation. This manipulation of other people's feelings is one of the worst places a person can be in. It is the worst place because it is an <u>intentional</u> attempt to use others for your own benefit. When you intentionally try to use others you are intentionally creating the need to use others in order to feel good about yourself.

To use others to make you feel good will simultaneously:

1) Feed your spirit
2) Perpetuate the need to manipulate others so you can feel good about yourself.

This makes your spirit much darker than it would be if you were not intentionally manipulating someone else's feelings.

When you embrace this darker reality and accept that you can do better you can begin to change your life.

Some people become consumed by having sympathy for everyone they meet. To over-emote in this way will not create a healthy spirit either. This overindulgence is only going to allow a person to feel something by using others to sympathize with them. When people use drama and trauma to over emote with an intention to encourage others to emote with you; you are using your emotions and spirit to manipulate others. When a person needs to be consumed in order to feel it is just a sign that their spirit needs some help.

I want to take a minute to state that people that overindulge or have any of the characteristics that this book describes as unhealthy are not doing anything wrong, per se. They are only living in the reality of their spirits existence. These behaviors are described to help to you recognize the signs and symptoms of an unhealthy spirit and soul.

If you over indulge you are either:

1) consumed by feelings and emotions
2) need to be consumed by your feelings and emotions

Please remember – the end game is a healthy spirit. With a healthy spirit you can allow love to flow through you. When you achieve this level of spiritual development you no longer need others to make you feel good; you just feel good. This is how you experience God's love flowing through you throughout your day-to-day life. This is the love that accompanies love-based consciousness. This love that does not encourage you to use others to make you feel good; it encourages you to do whatever you can to help others whether or not you receive anything for your effort. You may feel good about what you do or you may feel nothing from it; you may be paid for it or you may not. It is just about living with others in your life for the simple purpose of living. Life then creates its own happiness and joy.

These processes and forces of creation are not something you control. They are merely always at work around us creating lie's experiences that will encourage us to grow a healthier spirit and soul. This is how creation works and has been working to make our lives and spirit better from life-time to lifetime and generation to generation.

PART 4

CREATING COLLECTIVELY

THE INDIVIDUAL PERSON'S SPIRIT

THE COLLECITVE SPIRIT (GOD)

THE COLLECTIVE SPIRIT IN DARK (THE GOD OF THE DEAD)

THE COLLECTIVE SPIRIT IN LIGHT (THE GOD OF THE LIVING)

THE GENERATION GAP

There is an individual spirit and soul that experiences its existence in light or dark.

There is a collective spirit and consciousness that exists as the result of everyone's spirit and soul collectively.

There is an ambient or manifested spirit that exists in nature that is the result of what we create individually and collectively throughout our lives. The spirit of what we create and manifest throughout our lives has been in existence since the beginning of time. This ambient spirit lives and is continually re-created from generation to generation and life-time to life-time.

All three of these spiritual realities (individual spirit, collective spirit and ambient spirit) are nature and creation at work. After God's intention to create creation it was only natural that these would exist. Together they give us all the experiences that shape our personal lives and spiritual existence.

It is a very interactive system –we create them while they shape and create us.

Man's quest here on earth is to become one in body, spirit and soul individually and collectively. To that end God created the Kingdom of the Heavens (the Source of all emotions and consciousness). These Heavens are a place for our spirit and soul to exist while on this journey to heal our body, spirit and soul. These Heavens allow us to re-create our broken spirits and souls both individually and collectively. As our broken spirits and souls mend we will become one being of love and light in consciousness. After one person completes this process of carrying and resurrecting from his or her cross; he or she will become one in body, spirit and soul. As the result of having dealt with his or her issues (that are the cross) the quest to achieve enlightenment will have reached a milestone in our collective healing process and the end is near. This is the end of a time in creation. The end of an era in the evolution of man.

The end will not be here until everyone has completed this process of healing and become one being in love, light and consciousness. When individual consciousness has grown from the, "I Need" state of mind through the, "I Am", "We Are", "We are Us" we are approaching the end game of our quest to re-create our spirits and souls. The final phase of this evolution of the collective body, spirit and soul is becoming one in God consciousness in the "We Are God" reality.

We have talked a little bit about how the individual spirit and soul work together, now I would like to explain how these larger collective spirits and souls work to make society what it is today.

AN INDIVIDUAL PERSON'S SPIRIT

There are two different ways that spirit works. How a spirit that is capable of holding light works with the collective spirit of mankind is very different from how the same spirit which is not capable of holding light, works. Sincerity and insincerity are as different as night and day.

It is important to remember that we are here to facilitate the transformation of our spirit and soul from dark to light to God. Also it is important to remember that we are always feeding our spirit and soul as well as being fed by them. Changing the polarity of a person's spirit is a lot of hard work; there is no magic wand of intention that will transform your spirit.

In general terms an individual person's spirit and soul in light or in dark exist in basically the same way.

The spirit feeds a person the <u>feelings</u> that are associated with his or her intentions.

The soul feeds the person what he needs to <u>know</u> in order to accomplish his or her intentions.

A person with a spirit not capable of holding light will have a difficult time hearing thoughts that would ordinarily support a positive intention. This is because a darker spirit works to filter out thoughts and feelings that are lighter than the spirit is capable of holding.

But when it comes to the collective spirit in light or dark. The way many people's spirits interact with one another is different when a person's spirit is light or dark. A spirit not capable of holding light will interact in a very different way than a person's spirit that is capable of holding light. In a darker collective a person becomes part of a group or network of spirit that is of a similar vibration. This group or network feeds each other and feeds off of each other. While a spirit that is capable of holding light feeds off the love and light of the source of all feelings and emotions – the kingdom of the heavens. This is where a person with a pure spirit processes the pure love that comes from these heavens.

COLLECTIVE SPIRIT (GOD)

The collective spirit of mankind is what we think of as God. In this way there is a little bit of God in all of us. We are collectively evolving into a collective spirit that can hold light so we can live with love. This is why there is a little spark of light (God spark) in all of us. But we have to make that spark a reality. The healing processes discussed in this book explains how to create that spark and turn it into a blazing fire in your spirit and soul.

The collective spirit has been evolving throughout many life times and generations for thousands of years. It has a structure to it. Thousands of years ago that structure was by nations and tribes and people within a tribe and then the male or female gender of the person within the tribe. In the past there was not a sense of being a person; you were a member of a nation and tribe within that nation. In the structure that existed in the past your spirit was consumed by the spirit of the nation and tribe that you were born into. Today, there are probably many parts of the world in which this still exists. But it is changing; as it should. This structure was needed when the collective spirit of mankind existed in a darker reality. In order for people to survive they had to be a part of a larger group of people that could work together when necessary and fight to survive when needed. Today all around the world we are evolving into a person based reality where each of us has the opportunity to be who we are as an individual. The suppressive and controlling nature of living as a part of a nation that was separate from other nations no longer exists. We will grow into a collective spirit that will allow our spirits to be free to be what it should be – what it can be, what it is, who we are.

When we lived in the older top down structure all the people of the nation had to live with the same spirit. They were not allowed to think for themselves or do what they thought was best as an individual. The belief was that the survival of the nation depended on everyone contributing their spirit to the spirit of the nation.

The collective spirit of mankind is the sum total of all the spirit of everyone in the world. The collective spirit has many segments or subsets of it. One way to look at it is to think of two people that agree on something and have a strong commitment to what they are discussing. They become one in spirit as it relates to that particular subject matter. A small group of people that agree on a particular subject matter is an even larger subset of the collective spirit. The power of a group of 10 people that strongly agree on something; will create the spirit of their agreement, this will create a bond between them and create the spirit of that which they agree on. A community, city or state that agrees on something becomes an even greater force in creation. Thousands of years ago people were committed to their nations and tries and then national heritage and family. They lived within the constraints and limits of their family; this made the spirit of their family very strong. For many generations the commitment to marrying within a family or within a national heritage (like Germans only marrying other Germans or Italians only marrying other Italians) has shifted significantly. As people know longer view nationalities or race as a limitation to dating or being married, the collective spirit that has existed since the beginning of time has shifted. It is now rotating from being oriented vertically (top down) to horizontally.

Today the collective spirit is no longer seen as just a commitment to your family structure and nationality. Today it is more about your family, career, country and your belief in God. As time goes on the belief in one God or another God will eventually shift into an acceptance of one God. This will allow us all to better understand our collective spirit as the spirit that is all of mankind and how we can be controlled by it or use it collectively to make our lives better.

One way to look at the collective spirit is to perceive the spirit of the wealthy and the spirit of the middle class and the spirit of the rest of the people in the world. It is the spirit of greed that can exist at all levels of this world wide class structure. Greed is not about how much money someone has – Greed is about the need to have more of what you have (or perceive you do not have); the amount of greed in your life is a function of what you will do to have or take what you want and need. Generosity is the polar opposite of greed. Generosity is about what you will do for others and how deeply you will give to those that need or even give to those that may not need but only perceive the need to have. As gratefulness and generosity replace greed within the spirit of these social structures the world will naturally evolve into a better place.

Creating a spirit capable of holding light is the first step in making the world a better place. After reading this book you should know that forgiveness is the first step. Forgiving others that hurt you and seeking forgiveness from those that we hurt is only the first step. This step creates forgiveness in our individual spirits. When two people forgive one another they create a forgiving spirit within them and between themselves. Creating a forgiving spirit between two people is the next phase in this process of creation. The phase that will follow is when tribes and nations that have been hurting one another for thousands of years learn to forgive one another for their sins of the past. It is not about who did what to whom in the past that started the conflict. It is about all the hurt that both nations have done to one another as they strived to survive in a world with a collective spirit that was much darker than it is today. When America and Russia, Israel and Islam, religious institutions and all facets of the world that are challenged to love one another learn to forgive and love – THIS WORLD WILL HAVE THE OPPORTYUNITY TO BECOME A BETTER PLACE.

Our individual spirits, the collective spirit and the Kingdom of the heavens are all linked as one in creation. The kingdom of the heavens establishes a spiritual foundation though which our spirit exists and the reality that is our life is created. The collective spirit of mankind is the most powerful force in creation because it is the sum total of all our love and light, fears, anger and darkness. The most important reality in creation is that we are all connected and these collective forces of creation exist within us each and every minute of each and every day. How we manage the thoughts and feelings that come into our consciousness is what will determine the reality that is our lives.

THE COLLECTIVE SPIRIT IN DARK (THE GOD OF THE DEAD)

THE TRANSACTIONS AND EXCHANGES THAT CREATE A SPIRIT AT THE MOMENT OF CREATION

The collective spirit in dark is what some refer to as the God of the dead. When the collective spirit of mankind was dark many people wrote phrases in books like; we should fear God, God is a vengeful God or that God said we should kill animals and eat meat because he likes the smell of burning flesh. These references come from the Bible and were written in it about 3,700 years ago. When a person's spirit is not capable of holding light it is dead to creation. This is the best way to differentiate between the destructive based nature of mankind and creation based nature that we live in. Thousands of years ago the collective spirit of mankind was dead to creation.

When creating through an interaction with another person, a spiritual bond is created between the two people. Just like buying and selling something at the store is a transaction that exchanges goods and services. Our spirits can also make a transaction between the spirits of the people involved with an exchange. When anger, hatred, rage, jealousy or judgment are a part of an exchange; there is a price that we pay for these transactions. When people fear others they usually need to judge them in order to feel comfortable in their own skin. When a person judges another person he creates judgment in his or her personal spirit. Their spirit then feeds them the feeling or sensation of being judged.

There are many people in the world today that judge others. It is like a pool or ocean of emotion, intention and spirit that exists as a subset of the collective spirit of mankind. The deeper that your personal fears, anger, hatred or rage exist in your life the deeper you swim within this sea of fear and judgment. When a person swims in this sea of judgment he or she feels judged. It is like being judged by a jury of your own fears.

For example;

> If you have a low vibrating transaction there might be some disrespect exchanged. Disrespect creates an exchange that lowers your vibration. Then as a person lives with disrespect in his or her spirit they will then feel as if others do not respect them. Only by respecting others will they regain this feeling of self-respect.
>
> Many people struggle with the reality of judging others. They work hard to get past it but continue to catch themselves judging others. The good thing about this is that we are all working to make this change and it will create a better collective spirit. The thing to understand is that judgment exists in the air around us and keeps trying to feed off of us; thereby making us want to judge others. As we learn to accept others for who they are we will create and accepting spirit and lock the door to this pesky spirit that tries to enter our space. Not judging others will only cleanse our spirit of judgment; when we create acceptance in our spirit we will no longer have to worry about judging others.
>
> When someone feels rejected by others he or she will have to learn to accept others before this feeling of being rejected will be replaced by a feeling of acceptance. It is only by creating acceptance and respect for others in your spirit that you will feel accepted and respected by others.

There is always a price you pay for negative intentions but a positive intention is more like an investment that will pay dividends.
This exchange is what the third horseman of the prophecy Revelations is all about.

This exchange creates a spiritual bond between those involved with the transaction. When two people engage in the spirit of a conversation in which they both create the same rhythm and vibration (they have the same essence, intention and emotion) they create a spiritual bond. When two people share a positive loving exchange they will share the love and light of their spirit's with one another. This is a positive bond that will work in a symbiotic nature between the two bodies or hosts of this creation.

When a person with a negative spirit asserts his or her will over another person a different kind of bond occurs. A person, (a bully) with a spirit not capable of holding light, can make another person drop his or her countenance (aura; the light of your spirit); the exchange that will take place will create a parasitic bond for the person that has lost his or her light. This exchange is not one of sharing but of take and give. This is a transaction that has an intention to destroy the light in another person so the person with a darker spirit can control the person with a lighter spirit. This control comes in many forms today. As the person that was bullied ages, the control from this spiritual bond feels as if it is normal and natural. When a bond exists for many years it has been feeding itself off your spirit for so long that you do not realize that you have been compensating for it for all these years. People in this situation adjust their lives and cope with this connection as if it is the way it is supposed to be. When we realize this connection is not serving our best interest we can change this spiritual creation and release its grip on our life. The process of forgiveness and living with love will loosen this grip and transform this parasitic bond. The good news is that, today, there is enough love and light in the collective spirit of mankind that we can change this reality in the lives of our children. We are just beginning to recognize the destructive nature of these behaviors. The transformation of this spirit from a darker reality has begun.

A bully is anyone that attempts to force his or her will on another person by creating fear and anger in the other person. Through intimidation and aggression a person's countenance (aura) falls. A weaker spirit leaves a person susceptible to the will of an aggressor. When a person loses his or her love (his or her countenance falls) it is usually only a matter of time until this person is no longer capable of forgiving the hurtful acts of another. When this happens this person experiences anger, hatred or rage, as a parasitic bond is created. Simply by acting on these darker feelings you will create the bond that eventually will need to be re-created (forgiven).

At the moment in time when a bully, police officer, criminal, teacher, student, politician, manager, fellow employee, family member etc. takes the free will of another this darker bond in creation will exist. I hope you can see how asserting your will on others and doing hurtful things is just a state of nature that exists within people with a personal spirit not capable of holding light.

This process of destruction has existed in mankind's collective spirit and consciousness since the beginning of time and continues to grow and spread. At this point in time we have only just begun to collectively recognize that it exists. Through programs that empower children, women and citizens in general, we are just beginning to change the nature of this very powerful creation that survives and thrives in the collective spirit and consciousness of mankind.

As nations continue to transform themselves out of these darker spirits we will re-create this spirit of bullying and evolve into a better way of life. This better way of life will be a function of the way of life that we create collectively. As we transition from the era of individuals bullying one another and nations using empire building strategies to conquer one another; we are collectively creating a healthier love-based spirit and consciousness. To create this better way of life we all must be vigilant in practicing Forgiveness and continue to create through love and light.

When we create beyond forgiveness and love we are creating things like acceptance, mercy, faith, wisdom and more. We create these other aspects of who we are by using the same fundamental process that is used to create forgiveness in our spirit. The more love we put into accepting others the more acceptance we will create in our spirit. The more love we put into being merciful towards others the more mercy we will create in our spirit.

As we re-create this spirit of bullying it is important to remember that we should not just focus on what we do not want others to not do to us or our children; but to create the spirit of loving or mercy or acceptance towards one another that we want to replace bullying with.

After a child, or any other person, has been bullied they will lose the inner strength and power; this is the result of having their spirit broken. This weaker personal spirit will easily be overpowered by the darkness of this spirit of bullying. We need to raise our children to be stronger in spirit so they can stay focused in all the endeavors of their life. This is why we must all learn to turn the other cheek. As we turn the other cheek on bullies no matter what their age or who they are we will not allow the spirit of bullying to infect our lives. It is the fear that someone feels when bullied that will feed it. By not reacting to fear no matter how overpowering it is we will minimize its ability to feed off of us. When two people engage in an aggressive conversation they co-create a spiritual bond between one another. Bullying is a type of co-creation that makes a parasitic spiritual bond.

To only stop one group of people from bullying another will not transform the spirit of bullying; it will only allow this spirit to reshape itself. This is what is happening all throughout the world today. As people are demanding that teachers change their behavior in the classroom so their children will not feel bullied; many children and young men are feeling the power of the spirit of bullying in them and then react to that feel and bully their teachers. Since the teachers have been very effectively depowered and the spirit of bullying still exists in many classrooms, children are bullying teachers. All around the world this spirit of bullying is now able to infect children that are in classrooms. Instead of learning from their teachers they sense the spirit of bullying and then react to the anger within it. Any child that was bullied by a parent or taught to bully others by an adult (perhaps by a football or hockey coach that encourages over aggressiveness in a sport) will become susceptible to this spirit of bullying. When they feel the anger of this spirit they will naturally react to it in such a way as to attack their teachers.

When two people share a parasitic bond they are connected in spirit. This is a spiritual conduit that connects the spirit of two people. This spiritual connection to one another allows the essence of the spirit of one person to flow through this bond and into the other person. This spiritual exchange comes as a feeling that is similar to or exactly the same as the feeling that existed when the bond was created. When a person with anger hatred or rage transfers his or her anger to another person; the other person will naturally act on what he or she feels. This is the worst possible control that one person can have over another. Learning to not accept someone else's anger is the next step in mankind's collective evolution.

When a person has been bullied and loses his light, a part of his spirit joins the spirits of others that have been bullied. Those with the same fears swim in the sea of their fears. When a person's spirit is broken in this way and their spirit is sealed away from the sea that is filled with positive love based intentions and joins those that have been swimming in the sea of their fears. It is like they are locked or sealed away from the light and are given a key to this lesser light. This key unlocks the door to a room that will lead them to this sea where they can exist with the same spirit.

When a person's spirit is broken or shattered into many pieces he or she is no longer capable of feeling positive feelings or emotions. This creates a way of life that is designed to strive to survive with this darkness not thrive to live in light. This person's spirit will be like a cup half full of anger. Anger at this level (the cup is half full) is manageable in your day-to-day life. When your anger grows and your cup is full or begins to overflow, is when you need some relief from these feelings of rage, ire, disdain or wrath. This is the feeling of being in the abyss of your existence. When your cup overflows with these feelings you can no longer control them and you are forced to act on them. In this state of mind you are allowing your cup to be filled with the anger, hatred or rage that comes from that part of the collective spirit in which your personal spirit is a part of. It is like the collective spirit pours its anger into the cup that is your spirit.

This is when a person suddenly becomes a bully and creates a negative bond with someone else. The act of bullying creates a bond with this other person. In the future when the bully's cup overflows he will allow the bully's spirit to transfer some of his or her anger into the other person's spirit. Then this other person will act on his or her anger thereby spreading the negativity and the spirit of bullying to others. This continues until a network is created and then a group or gang is created. This group or gang can share the anger that exists within all of them; passing anger to one another in an attempt to manage the overall anger, hatred and rage they now live with individually and collectively. When one person feels as if his cup is overflowing he can then transfer that feeling to someone in his gang who will then allow his or her cup to fill a little while allowing the first person's cup to lower its level of anger. When something extremely traumatic happens to someone or several people in the gang everyone's cup can overflow simultaneously. This is when a group or gang acts out in a very aggressive way. This overwhelming feeling occurs when their collective spirits become consumed by the actions of another. When their cups overflow in this manner they have only two options:

1) Grow a larger cup of anger. When a person or group of people feel powerless against a larger bully and cannot let their rage out they can only exist with their anger, hatred and rage. This will create a larger cup to hold the darkness of the anger in their sprit. Eventually this leads to a larger network of others that are needed to transfer anger throughout them.

2) Act on their feelings. They are not going to be capable of lowering the level of anger in their spirit until they do something to get rid of it. When a child or young man feels as if he has nowhere to go with his spirit he will act on what he feels. In an attempt to control these feelings he or she might become aggressive with others, exercise, gamble, work harder, do drugs and alcohol or use sex to try to remove the anger from his or her spirit. This will lower the anger in his spirit thereby allowing him to present himself in a manner more acceptable to society or his social group.

When people learn to recognize that anger is not something they have to own they can learn to reject it. First they have to sense that it is there and then they have to send it back to its owner. Since all spirit is created from thoughts, words and actions, a simple thought that says, "I don't want this anger in me please return to your owner" will send it packing. This thought is not a simple comment; you have to mean it, you have to put a lot of emotions and truly want it to go away; and it will. There are many ways to not allow anger to manifest within you. You only have to be creative with how you send it back with peace and love to its originator.

The key characteristics to this process of rejecting someone else's anger are

1) Be strong in your Will to reject it; you have to really mean it
2) Send as much positive energy as you can with it; do not volley their anger.

Varying degrees of anger feel acceptable to those that live with anger. When a person lives with a certain level of anger he or she will probably not sense the same level of anger in someone else (unless intentionally trying to sense it). This is how social groups are formed. People are attracted to others that are of the same spirit. But, you do have to be careful of some people though. There are those that try to use groups with lighter spirits than their own so they can feel better about themselves. These are the manipulators and deceivers discussed earlier in this book. For the most part people feel more comfortable socializing with groups that are of a similar spiritual nature as themselves.

Some people with darker spirits often attempt to join groups that have lighter spirits. They attempt to deceive or manipulate their way into the group, create bonds with those within the group and then try to feed off the light of those in the group. When the members of the group realize their light is being manipulated they act in such a way as to root out the person with the darker spirit. The challenge they face is that their spirits are now of a lower vibration. This lower vibration is a reality that exists because the person with a darker spirit has co-created with them and this will lower their vibration. This means their ability to perceive and identify the manipulator is not as strong as it was before infected by this other person. The manipulator is accepted into the group and his or her spirit works in such a way as to hide its self while creating anger and dissension within the group. The more this group strives to identify the manipulator the more the spirit of the manipulator works to hide itself throughout the rest of the group. This makes others present themselves in the wrong way as they act on the anger that comes from within the group. The manipulator will destroy the group before leaving it or the group will rekindle its light thereby making the manipulator feel uncomfortable and it will leave them alone. A manipulator will not want to feel the love of the group, he or she will only want to use the spirit of the group to make him-self or her-self feel better when his or her cup overflows with anger.

EVERY NATION IN THE WORLD HAS ITS OWN SPIRIT WITH ITS OWN CHARACTERISTICS

A lot of people all throughout the world can recognize that there is a difference between the cultures of different nations. Some say one nation is too passive while they will also say that another nation is too aggressive. Most people refer to these differences as cultural differences. Actually they are the collective spiritual differences that are created by the people of the country. The way their governments' regulate laws and the people respond to meet (or to not meet) the intentions of these laws will all have an impact on the spirit they create. As the United Nations works to create peaceful solutions to global conflicts the world will slowly but surely grow into a more peaceful collective spirit. We need that governing body to continually prod all nations to strive to create peace. As we all learn to control our personal spirits and to deal with the issues that create our anger, hatred and rage, we will create a world that finds its path to peace and love.

In every large group or organization there are at least two realities in spirit. There is the spirit of the organization and then there is the spirit of the people within it. For example there is the spirit of a religious organization and then there is the spirit of the congregation. They are rarely the same.

We are creating more peace and more love each and every day. We just have to continue to recognize when we experience anger and then work to identify its source either within us or from an external source and then correct it. Forgive, Forgive, Forgive and then Forgive again.

THE COLLECTIVE SPIRIT IN LIGHT (THE GOD OF THE LIVING)

When two or more people live with light in their spirit they share the love that is in their hearts. They share this love with each other and many others all throughout their lives. This exchange is a sharing that is mutual. It feels just as good to give as to receive. When two people are drawn to both give and receive they have balance. Balance comes from sharing and having no expectation of receiving anything from one another; it is about simply being grateful for what they have and the opportunity to share who they are and what they have (their light).

As I am writing this book I am simply grateful to have the chance to share what I know with you. I have no expectation of myself that the information is perfect or that it has to be perfect. In this mind set I have no expectations that will limit my ability to receive this information from the spirit and soul of creation. Therefore I can be grateful for what I receive and let my intention to learn the truth about creation come through me. Because of this state of mind I have learned that creation is sharing its message through me. Part of this message is to give mankind what it needs to know at this moment in our spiritual evolution. This means that sometime in the future an even deeper understanding of creation will be shared through someone else. As the collective spirit of mankind evolves what we need to know will be there in our consciousness for us. You see the same message comes from creation. As mankind's collective spirit becomes cleanses its self the message is received with greater clarity and the information received will be perfect for those that receive it. As a person cleanses his or her spirit he or she will receive a different message because they are being told what they need to know when they need to know it. This is the perfection of creation.

Does this mean that what I am writing today is wrong? I am not sure – I guess that is up to the reader to decide.

Many people believe that giving of themselves completely is enough; it is not. You must let others do for you as well as do for others. It is not like buying and selling; it is not about getting your money's worth or the value of a trade. When two people exchange love and light the value is in the exchange not in the amount of love or light that one person gives and the other receives. Creation is in the acceptance of the exchange not the amount that one person gives or the other receives. The exchange is so cool because when you send love to someone else you will feel the love flow through you. This is what it is all about; this is why you need a spirit capable of holding light and you have to learn to allow it to flow through you. When you get to the point where you no longer try to assess whether you gave enough or received enough with every interaction you experience; a sense of peace will enter your spirit and you will know that you have balance in your relationships. Acceptance of yourself and others will just naturally be a part of this phase of your personal growth and development. As the world grows into a state of acceptance we will all feel so much more comfortable in our own lives.

Please Remember – When you live with expectations it is because you created expectations in your spirit. People create expectations through a need to have things and people in your life. To create acceptance in your spirit you have to:

1) learn to no longer expect anything from others
2) allow yourself to be generous and grateful in every transaction you have in your life

When two people exchange light between themselves the spirit of their thoughts, words and actions impact the collective spirit of themselves first and then the network of friends they associate with. When a group of people work together for a common cause or purpose the spirit of their thoughts words and actions will impact the collective spirit of a larger group (perhaps the city, state or nation they are in) of the collective spirit of mankind.

It is like lighting a match or candle in a room that has no light in it. The entire room is affected by that one single flame. That part of the room that is closest to the flame is impacted in a greater way than a part of the room that is farthest from the flame. As two people share their flames a fire is ignited that will have an even greater impact on the collective spirit of mankind.

As more people create a flame in their life and share that flame with others the light of the world will be ignited. As more people join this creation of light they will shine like blazing lamps of fire burning bright that will shine on mountain tops for all to see. This will impact everyone not just those that have a light spirit. It will make many people sense and feel their own light or lack of light thereby encouraging more people to find their quest for light as they pick-up their cross and walk their walk. People that are motivated to start their quest might experience a lot of anger when exposed to the reality of a greater light in the collective spirit of mankind. When people live with a darker spirit, the anger in their spirit will naturally be triggered when they are exposed to this higher light in the world. Remember anger is their primary response to any and all emotions. Therefore, when they sense someone with a light spirit in their presence they can only sense and feel their anger they will react to their feelings just like anyone else. They may even feel exposed as to who they are as if they can no longer hide the true spirit of whom they are and this will make them angry. Just accept them for who they are and be there for them when they need your help and assistance while carrying their cross.

As an individual person creates a spirit capable of holding light he or she will become more sensitive to

1) Feeling the ambient spirit that is in the air around us.
2) They will become more sensitive to the feelings of others.
3) Even more sensitive to what they read in an email, see on television or hear on the radio.

As the collective spirit of mankind continues to grow into the light everyone will feel more sensitive to the spirit of the thoughts, words and actions of others. As we grow collectively in this way, we will all become more sensitive and follow the lead of those that made the first steps into the light.

One final thought on the collective light of the spiritual world. As the light in our collective spirit grows it is only natural that we will all become more powerful creators. This means that the intentions behind our thoughts words and actions will have a greater impact on our-self and others. The emotion behind our thoughts, words and actions will have a greater impact on our-self and others. The essence of who we are (in light or in dark) will have a greater impact on us. To be more specific, this means not only will the power of people with a light spirit be greater in creation but also the power of people with negative intentions and the essence through which they create will be stronger.

THE GENERATION GAP

HOW WE COLLECTIVELY RE-CREATE THE WORLD LIFE-TIME AFTER LIFE-TIME, GENERATION AFTER GENERATION

Life-time after life-time we individually re-create our-selves.

Generation by generation we collectively re-create this world and the spirit of it.

We make this world a better place each and every day we are alive and live with love in our hearts.

As a generation of children enter the world, we come with a collective spirit that is greater than the spirit of the generation that came before us and greater than the collective spirit of mankind at that point in time. This collective spirit of the world is constantly being impacted by the love and light of the children that incarnate with this love, light and a purpose to make the changes the world needs. Even if this love and light is immature it will bring a higher light into the world as these children grow into adults a more mature love develops.

The power of prayer is an incredible reality in our lives. The generations come into the world with a purpose to create specific changes. These changes are the changes the previous generations want to see in the world. When we pray or have a deep seeded feeling that is directed with a thought that you think will make the world a better place; the spirit of these prayers or deep seeded feelings are created. Those thoughts and feelings exist in spirit and want to live. They connect to the same or similar thoughts and feelings that come from others. Then as they grow into their own reality they become the purpose of future generations of people and children that come into the world.

In the early 1900's the world was experiencing the First World War. During and after this war people from all around the world were scared about what was happening in the world. They prayed and felt deeply about all the wrongs that were related to this war. They did not have to talk to each other in order to share a common feeling and desire to stop all the conflict in the world; they merely had to feel a desire to make this change. These desires and fears came together to manifest the purpose of the next three generations that came into the world. The first generation grew up to fight against Hitler. The collective spirit of the world came together to stop Hitler. We impacted the world in a very profound way because we changed this ago old spirit that existed for thousands of years. Our actions changed the spirit of the primary motivator that existed in the ambient spirit of the world. It changed the spirit of the empire building strategies and bullying that plagued mankind for more thousands of years. Stopping the empire building strategy also stopped the bullying spirit that was attached to the spirit of these wars and the empire building way of life. This changed the spirit of the world and now allows people to feel free to explore more peaceful ways of life. This generation came together collectively motivated to stop Hitler from accomplishing his objective to conquer the world. When we all came together for this common purpose we began to create a shift in the ambient spirit of the world. The next generation brought with it the peace and love of the hippie movement. Stopping the spirit of the empire building mentality and then replacing it with the spirit of peace and love is probably the most profound spiritual changes this world has seen in its history. Today the impact of these two generations has brought a feeling of freedom in to the lives of people all around the world. The freedom to take charge of our lives and the lives of those we love are seen in the movements to stop bullying in all its shapes and forms and to strive to make peace on earth. Remember peace on earth begins with my peace of mind. As younger generations continue to create this new world order we will create a better world. The first two generations re-created the spirit of empire building and the second generation infused it with a loving spirit and soul. Now the youth of today can make a new reality in the world because they live in a world with a spirit that is not as oppressive. They are not as consumed by the same reality that existed in the 1940's and 1950's; this frees there soul to make the world a better place. Now they have to do it and the older generations have to support them.

We may not be there yet but we are definitely on the right path.

IN SUMMARY

This book has introduced you to creation and the natural cycle of life that begins with a child's spirit in love and light. We have discussed how a child loses his or her love as he or she learns to live with a spirit that exists without light. Then life becomes a quest to find your light again; to rekindle the flame that once existed in your spirit, the flames that fueled your soul and its connection to love and the consciousness that comes with love and light.

This story of life and creation is also the story of the prophecy "The Revelation of Christ" and the parables that are written in the King James Holy Bible's New Testament. Revelations has been viewed by many as having a destructive nature. This is true. It is about the destructive nature of God which is the destructive nature of mankind collectively, when the vision came to St. John. At that point in time, St John had a vision that represented what mankind's collective spirit had created over the past 2,000 years. It is the destructive nature of creation when our spirits are not capable of holding light that was seen in his vision.

An example of how this book explains the story of Revelations is best explained through the infamous four horsemen of the apocalypse. These four horse men are part of an image in the prophecy that is seen as seven seals that seal a book. This book of knowledge is the consciousness that is available to mankind when these seals are released (they are released when we experience the process of forgive and live with love). When the seals are released we are capable of allowing love-based consciousness into our lives. The four horsemen are described as:

1) A rider on a white horse that is being handed a crown and sets out conquering and to conquer.
2) A rider on a red horse that takes peace from the world.
3) A rider on a black horse that is carrying a scale an in the background is the sounds of men negotiating about buying and selling food.
4) A rider on a pale horse named death followed closely by Hades.

These four horses explain the process of losing our light. The first horseman represents a person giving away his or her light (and the power and authority that comes with the wisdom of your love and light) to someone that takes it.

The second horseman represents how a person now lives without a spirit that holds light. This leads you to become just like the bully that took your crown as your loss of peace of mind puts you on a path to take peace from others.

The third is the transaction and exchange that occurs when a person loses his or her light. Just like buying and selling goods and services we all learn to swap the negativity of our spirit from person to person.

The fourth is the progression of our spirit into the darkness of the abyss and how the soul will follow the spirit. The death of the spirit will always lead to the soul creating through the darkness of the abyss of Hades. When the spirit losses its light it is dead to creation. Where the spirit goes the soul will follow and the process of creation will reflect the light or dark of the spirit and soul.

This part of the prophecy is about how we all learn to create hell on earth.

The moral of this part of the story is that we can:

1) Ride the fear and anger, wants and needs, desires and cravings of these horses wildly into the darkness of our abyss, or

2) We can tame them from within through the process of forgiving and living with love and walk them peacefully into the light of life.

One of the first parables that Jesus talks about in the book of Matthew is about the bride groom leaving the brides chamber. Then later towards the end of parables in the book of Matthew are a series of parables that talk about marriage. The entire book of Matthew (as wells the other books written by Mark, Luke and John) all tell the story of creation from the perspective of this spiritual healing process. The parable of the bride groom leaving the brides chamber is about the separation of spirit and soul. The soul is the bride groom and the spirit is the bride's chamber. Later in the book of Matthew the parables talk about preparing the bride and groom for the wedding; these parables are about the spirit and soul becoming one again. This union is the holiest of all unions and only comes to fruition as the result of people healing people and working together as we all strive to survive until we learn to thrive with love. The process of Forgive and Live with Love is what Revelations refers to as Repent and Overcome. The first scene of the prophecy talks about seven churches which are the states of mind (wrath, greed, lust, gluttony, sloth, pride and envy) discussed earlier. In order to transform our spirit and soul we have to learn to forgive and live with love so we can transform the nature of the beast that resides inside each of us individually and all of us collectively. This beast is the essence of the wants and needs, desires and cravings that control our lives and motivate us to act through the darker spirits of wrath, greed, lust etc. The beast represents people that are consumed by or live in the belly of the beast as they strive to survive.

Once we have created Forgiveness in our spirit we can live with light in our spirit and love in our hearts. With forgiveness in our spirit we will naturally have this feeling of wanting to do something with the love and light that comes with it. When people get to this point in the healing process they search for a purpose in their life, many will search for God's purpose for them. The interesting thing about life and God's purpose for us is that we forgive so we can find our love and light. This is God's purpose for all of us. When most people are searching for this sense of purpose we have already done it. Then all we have to do is live with purpose. Living with purpose and finding purpose in life is what the third scene in Revelations is about. In this third scene there is a woman about to give birth and a dragon waiting to consume to her child, seven angels filled with plagues holding seven cups and then a woman on a beast holding a cup that is full of idolatrous pollutions, and the impurities of her lewdness. This scene is about

1) Future generations of children coming into the world

2) Future generations having a greater light and purpose in their life

3) Being consumed by the lifestyle that existed in the world (the dragon)

4) Living our lives consumed by the spirit of that which existed before we came into the world and being consumed by the our past life issues that will become a part of our reality in this life-time

When Jesus was being taken by the chief priest to be tried by the Jewish leaders his friend and disciple Peter cut off the ear of the chief priest that came to arrest him. After Jesus healed the ear of the Chief Priest he asked Peter to put way his sword and said "The <u>cup</u> that the Father has given me, shall I not drink it?" In this statement he is saying that it is his purpose to be tried and to die for his convictions and beliefs – therefore he must drink from his cup or complete his purpose.

When a person lives with a spirit that is not capable of holding light he lives with a purpose (or cup) that is overflowing. Another image in this third scene of the prophecy is of a woman on a beast holding a cup filled with the idolatrous pollutions of the world. The name of this woman is Babylon. She is consumed by the essence of greed, lust and gluttony, sloth, pride and envy. This is a reflection of the darker way of life that existed when the vision came to St. John. When the prophecy talks about Babylon it is referring to the events and lifestyle that created the spirit of the gluttonous and lustful nature of mankind.

But the good news is that seven angels will blow seven trumpets bringing with them that which is needed to rekindle the fire within our spirits as we transform our darkness into light. As we learn to tame those wild horses from within we will regain our peace of mind. Remember peace on earth always begins with one person finding his or her peace of mind.

There is another image in the prophecy that is so beautiful – it is a woman about to give birth to a child and a dragon waiting to consume that child. This woman giving birth to a child is Mother Nature giving birth to the spirit and soul of future generations of children. The dragon waiting to consume this child is the collective spirit of mankind waiting to consume and be consumed by these children; as the two integrate into one spirit that will be better than it was before these children were born. Then there are two beasts that are seen, they represent the lifetimes where these children live and deal with their issues in life thereby cleansing the ambient spirit that exists in the world and making the world a better place for future generations to live in.

The final scene of the prophecy is about the New Holy City of Jerusalem. This is the final part of our body, spirit and souls journey into the kingdom of God. This state of mind is when the essence of who we are becomes one with our spirit and soul. As the healing process that we have experienced for many lifetimes becomes complete our spirit and soul are no longer separate from one another. This one-ness that we become is the end result of all the work that we do through that which the Creator created in the beginning.

As we become one in love, light and consciousness we are completing the healing of our bodies, spirits and souls. As our spirits and souls have learned to feed off love, light and consciousness we will integrate into one body, spirit and soul – life time after life time, generation after generation. This being that we become is a state of consciousness that is like being connected to a stream of consciousness that becomes us. We are now complete as we live, love and laugh knowing that all is good again.

With Love, Light and Peace

Phoenix